What Do You Know
About the Bible?

the New Testament

What Do You Know About the Bible?

the New Testament

Carolyn Tynes-Turner, Ph.D. (Education)

Publication assistance by

PAGEMASTER
PUBLISHING
PageMaster.ca

Special Dedication

My loving parents, Walter (Jack) and Sadie Tynes taught me about God, our Lord Jesus Christ, and Christian Scriptures. In various ways, they introduced me to the Bible early in my life and encouraged me to read it regularly to develop faith in the Lord and find comfort during life's struggles. Thus, I am grateful for our family devotions and my parents' consistent example of daily Bible reading, where I learned to seek the Scriptures. I dedicate this book to them.

Contents

Follow these steps:

1.   Read one chapter at a time.

2.   Write the answers to the questions on the lines.

3.   Check the answers in the *Questions/Answers* section.

4.   There is no need to flip back to the questions; this section contains the questions and answers.

5.   Check the references for further study, and take notes on the key points.

6.   Record your score.

The author used the King James Version in compiling the questions and answers. However, consult any version of the Bible to find the answers. Designed to challenge and teach, *What Do You Know About the Bible? The New Testament* will inspire further study and strengthen your faith in God. Enjoy the quiz!

To submit questions or feedback, please do not hesitate to contact Carolyn Tynes-Turner.

email:
cannturner@gmail.com

Introduction

How many lepers did Jesus heal on his way to Jerusalem? Who received the key of "the bottomless pit"? How did John the Baptist die, and what did his disciples do with his body? If you would like to find answers to Bible questions like these, this is the book for you.

Learning about the Bible is a goal many people desire to achieve; however, accomplishing this objective often becomes challenging. The question and answer format of this book offers a systematic way for Bible lovers to learn about the Bible in a captivating way and focus on the spiritual messages of the passages. You will be astounded at how much you learn and walk away with a hunger to discover more truths in the Scriptures.

This book consists of 260 questions and answers to challenge your Bible knowledge and teach more about the characters, places, and events of The New Testament. The chronological order of the book makes it easy to follow the events as they happened and better understand the passages.

*Read **The Book of Matthew** before continuing.*

Questions - The Book of Matthew

Q 1.   (Matthew 1) What is the interpretation of the name Emmanuel?

_____

_____

_____

Q 2.   (Matthew 2) Which king ruled at the time of Jesus' birth in Bethlehem, and why did he assemble the chief priests and scribes?

_____

_____

_____

Q 3.   (Matthew 3) Where did John the Baptist preach, and which prophet foretold John's ministry?

_____

_____

_____

Q 4.   (Matthew 4) By the Sea of Galilee, which men did Jesus call to follow Him, and what were they doing?

_____

_____

_____

Q 5.   (Matthew 5) Seeing a multitude of people, Jesus ascended a mountain. When he sat down, the disciples joined him. What did Jesus do next?

_____

_____

_____

Q 6.   (Matthew 6) What did Jesus teach about treasures on earth and in Heaven?

_____

_____

_____

Q 7.   (Matthew 7) Jesus told several parables in Matthew Chapter 7. After Jesus spoke these parables, what astonished the people about His teachings?

_____

_____

_____

Q 8.   (Matthew 8) Why did the centurion seek Jesus, and how did Jesus respond?

_____

_____

_____

Q 9.   (Matthew 9) Who touched the hem of Jesus' garment?

_____

_____

_____

Q 10.   (Matthew 10) How many disciples did Jesus call?

_____

_____

_____

Q 11.   (Matthew 11) While in prison, what did John the Baptist do upon hearing of Christ's works and preaching in the cities?

_____

_____

_____

Q 12.   (Matthew 12) Jesus went into the synagogue and encountered a man
with a withered hand. After telling the man to stretch out his hand,
Jesus restored the man's hand. What did the Pharisees do?

_____

_____

_____

Q 13.   (Matthew 13) In the parable of the sower, what happened to the
seeds that fell on good ground?

_____

_____

_____

Q 14.   (Matthew 14) How did John the Baptist die, and what did his
disciples do with his body?

_____

_____

_____

Q 15.   (Matthew 15) Jesus performed a miracle and fed a multitude of four
thousand who had not eaten in three days. What did Jesus feed the
multitude, and what was left?

_____

_____

_____

Q 16.   (Matthew 16) To tempt Jesus, what did the Pharisees and Sadducees
ask Him to show them, and what did He tell them about seeking a
sign?

_____

_____

_____

Q 17.   (Matthew 17) Who did Jesus take to His transfiguration, and where
did they go?

_____

_____

_____

Q 18.   (Matthew 18) How did Jesus respond when the disciples asked,
        "Who is the greatest in the kingdom of heaven" (Matthew 18:1
        KJV)?

        _____

        _____

        _____

Q 19.   (Matthew 19) What did the young man seek when he came to Jesus,
        and why did Jesus' response cause the young man to feel sorrow?

        _____

        _____

        _____

Q 20.   (Matthew 20) In the parable of the labourers in the vineyard, how
        much did the householder agree to pay the labourers?

        _____

        _____

        _____

Q 21.   (Matthew 21) As Jesus came to the fig tree, what did He find, and
        what eventually happened to the tree?

        _____

        _____

        _____

Q 22.   (Matthew 22) To deceive Jesus, what did the Pharisees ask, and how
        did they react to His response?

        _____

        _____

        _____

Q 23.   (Matthew 23) Jesus condemned the works of the Pharisees. What
        did Jesus say about their works and outward appearances?

        _____

        _____

        _____

Q 24.   (Matthew 24) At the Mount of Olives, what did the disciples ask Jesus? How did Jesus answer the disciples' question?

_____

_____

_____

Q 25.   (Matthew 25) Jesus told a parable of ten virgins. How did five virgins behave wisely, and how did five behave foolishly on their way to meet the bridegroom?

_____

_____

_____

Q 26.   (Matthew 26) What did a woman pour on Jesus' head at Simon the leper's home in Bethany?

_____

_____

_____

Q 27.   (Matthew 27) Who was Joseph of Arimathaea, and what did Joseph do after he begged Jesus' body?

_____

_____

_____

Q 28.   (Matthew 28) What time did Mary Magdalene and Mary go to the sepulcher, and what did the angel of the Lord tell the women?

_____

_____

_____

Score: /28 points

Reflection and Prayer - the Book of Matthew

Reflect on Chapters 1-28, and choose one verse that speaks to your heart. Write the verse.

Prayer: Write a prayer asking God to help you apply the verse to situations in your own life.

*Read **The Book of Mark** before continuing.*

Questions - The Book of Mark

Q 1.   (Mark 1) Who did John baptize in the wilderness?

_____

_____

_____

Q 2.   (Mark 2) Who was Levi's father, and where did Jesus see Levi and
        invite him to follow Him?

_____

_____

_____

Q 3.   (Mark 3) What did Jesus surname Simon?

_____

_____

_____

Q 4.   (Mark 4) In the parable of the sower, what happened to the seeds
        that fell into the thorns?

_____

_____

_____

Q 5.   (Mark 5) Jesus healed a man who had an unclean spirit then
        permitted the unclean spirits to enter a herd of swine that ran into
        the ocean and drowned. What was the man like afterward?

_____

_____

_____

Q 6.   (Mark 6) What happened when Jesus went to His own country and taught in the synagogue?

_____

_____

_____

Q 7.   (Mark 7) Jesus healed a deaf man who had a speech impediment. What did Jesus do that showed the man his healing came from God?

_____

_____

_____

Q 8.   (Mark 8) Which events did Jesus foretell of His suffering, and how did Peter respond?

_____

_____

_____

Q 9.   (Mark 9) Was Peter present at Jesus' transfiguration?

_____

_____

_____

Q 10.   (Mark 10) Who was Bartimaeus, and where was he when Jesus passed by?

_____

_____

_____

Q 11.   (Mark 11) Whose tables and chairs did Jesus overthrow in the Temple?

_____

_____

_____

Q 12.   (Mark 12) What was the value of two mites?

_____

_____

_____

Q 13.   (Mark 13) Finish this verse: "Heaven and earth shall pass away:" /
        (Mark 13:31 KJV).

_____

_____

_____

Q 14.   (Mark 14) Although the chief priests and scribes wanted to put Jesus
        to death, why did they not choose to put Him to death during the
        Passover and the Feast of Unleavened Bread?

_____

_____

_____

Q 15.   (Mark 15) At Jesus' crucifixion, the soldiers impelled Simon to
        carry Jesus' cross. Who was Simon?

_____

_____

_____

Q 16.   (Mark 16) What did the women bring to the sepulcher, and what did
        they find?

_____

_____

_____

Score: /16 points

Reflection and Prayer-The Book of Mark

Reflect on Chapters 1-16, and choose one verse that speaks
to your heart. Write the verse.

*Prayer: Write a prayer asking God to help you apply
the verse to situations in your own life.*

*Read **The Book of Luke** before continuing.*

Questions - The Book of Luke

Q 1.   (Luke 1) What happened after Zacharias wrote "His name is John" on a tablet (Luke 1:63)?

_____

_____

_____

Q 2.   (Luke 2) Who was Anna, and what did she do daily and nightly?

_____

_____

_____

Q 3.   (Luke 3) Why did Herod place John the Baptist in prison; what were the names of Herod's brother and his wife?

_____

_____

_____

Q 4.   (Luke 4) How long did Jesus spend in the wilderness?

_____

_____

_____

Q 5.   (Luke 5) Where was Levi when Jesus invited him to follow Him, and what did Levi do after following Jesus?

_____

_____

_____

Q 6.   (Luke 6) One day, Jesus chose twelve disciples. What did Jesus do before He chose the disciples, and what did He call them?

_____

_____

_____

Q 7.   (Luke 7) At Capernaum, why did a centurion send his elders to Jesus, and what did Jesus do?

_____

_____

_____

Q 8.   (Luke 8) Why did Jairus fall at the feet of Jesus?

_____

_____

_____

Q 9.   (Luke 9) Describe Jesus' countenance at His transfiguration.

_____

_____

_____

Q 10.   (Luke 10) Who was Martha's sister, and what did the sisters do when Jesus visited Martha's house?

_____

_____

_____

Q 11.   (Luke 11) Jesus cast out a dumb devil. What did the devil do?

_____

_____

_____

Q 12.   (Luke 12) Jesus told a parable of a rich fool. What message did Jesus reveal at the end of the parable?

_____

_____

_____

Q 13.   (Luke 13) What did the woman with a spirit of infirmity do when Jesus spoke healing words and laid hands on her?

_____

_____

_____

Q 14.   (Luke 14) Where and when did Jesus encounter a man who had dropsy?

_____

_____

_____

Q 15.   (Luke 15) In the parable of the lost sheep, how many sheep did the man have, and how many did he lose? How did the man respond upon finding the lost sheep?

_____

_____

_____

Q 16.   (Luke 16) Jesus told a parable about a rich man and his steward. What accusation did the rich man make toward his steward?

_____

_____

_____

Q 17.   (Luke 17) How many lepers did Jesus heal on His way to Jerusalem?

_____

_____

_____

Q 18.   (Luke 18) Jesus told a parable about a widow and a judge. What did the widow ask the judge, and how did the judge respond?

_____

_____

_____

Q 19.   (Luke 19) Who was Zacchaeus, and how did he get to see Jesus?

_____

_____

_____

Q 20.   (Luke 20) Who sent spies to deceive Jesus, and why?

_____

_____

_____

Q 21.   (Luke 21) Jesus taught in the Temple during the day. Where did He
        go at night?

_____

_____

_____

Q 22.   (Luke 22) At Jesus' betrayal, what happened when one with Jesus
        struck the servant, cutting off his right ear?

_____

_____

_____

Q 23.   (Luke 23) What did Pilate do upon hearing that Jesus was a
        Galilaean, and where was Herod at the time?

_____

_____

_____

Q 24.   (Luke 24) What happened as two disciples walked toward Emmaus, and how far was it from Jerusalem?

_____

_____

_____

Score: /24 points

Reflection and Prayer-The Book of Luke

Reflect on Chapters 1-24, and choose one verse that speaks to your heart. Write the verse.

Prayer: Write a prayer asking God to help you apply the verse to situations in your own life.

*Read **The Book of John** before continuing.*

Questions - The Book of John

Q 1.   (John 1) The Pharisees asked John the Baptist why he baptized if he were not Christ, Elias (Elijah), or the prophet. How did John show humility toward Christ?

_____

_____

_____

Q 2.   (John 2) At the marriage in Cana of Galilee, how many waterpots needed filling?

_____

_____

_____

Q 3.   (John 3) How did Nicodemus know that God had sent Jesus to teach and perform miracles?

_____

_____

_____

Q 4.   (John 4) What first influenced the Samaritans to believe in Christ, and how long did Jesus remain with them?

_____

_____

_____

Q 5.   (John 5) Where was the pool containing five porches, and what was the pool called?

_____

_____

_____

Q 6.   (John 6) How far had the disciples rowed before seeing Jesus
        walking on the sea, and how did they feel upon seeing Jesus?

_____

_____

_____

Q 7.   (John 7) Who came to see Jesus at night?

_____

_____

_____

Q 8.   (John 8) The scribes and Pharisees brought a woman who had
        committed adultery to Jesus. What did they say?

_____

_____

_____

Q 9.   (John 9) The Pharisees asked the blind man how he received his
        sight. How did the blind man reply, and on which day did the blind
        man's healing occur?

_____

_____

_____

Q 10.   (John 10) What reason did the Jews give for wanting to stone Jesus?

_____

_____

_____

Q 11.   (John 11) How long was Lazarus dead before Jesus raised him?

_____

_____

_____

Q 12.   (John 12) The Greeks came to worship at a feast. What request did
        the Greeks make of Philip, and where was Philip's home?

_____

_____

_____

Q 13.   (John 13) Who did Jesus give the sop?

_____

_____

_____

Q 14.   (John 14) Jesus told the disciples that knowing Him meant knowing the Father. Who asked Jesus to show them the Father?

_____

_____

_____

Q 15.   (John 15) Jesus told His disciples he called them "friends," not servants. Why?

_____

_____

_____

Q 16.   (John 16) Who did Jesus say He would send when He went away?

_____

_____

_____

Q 17.   (John 17) What was Jesus' prayer for His disciples?

_____

_____

_____

Q 18.   (John 18) How did Annas send Jesus to Caiaphas?

_____

_____

_____

Q 19.   (John 19) Who commanded the soldiers to scourge Jesus?

_____

_____

_____

Q 20.   (John 20) Which items did Simon Peter see in the sepulcher, and how were they arranged? What was the reaction of Peter and the other disciple that arrived?

_____

_____

_____

Q 21.   (John 21) After Jesus' resurrection, where did He reveal Himself to the disciples?

_____

_____

_____

Score: /21 points

Reflection and Prayer-The Book of John

Reflect on Chapters 1-21, and choose one verse that speaks to your heart. Write the verse.

Prayer: Write a prayer asking God to help you apply the verse to situations in your own life.

*Read **The Book of Acts** before continuing.*

Questions - The Book of Acts

Q 1.   (Acts 1) How did the disciples choose Matthias to become an apostle?

_____

_____

_____

Q 2.   (Acts 2) On the Day of Pentecost, what amazed the multitudes?

_____

_____

_____

Q 3.   (Acts 3) What did the lame man at the gate called Beautiful do after Peter healed him?

_____

_____

_____

Q 4.   (Acts 4) Who was Joses (Joseph), and what did he do among the community of believers?

_____

_____

_____

Q 5.   (Acts 5) Who were Ananias and Sapphira, and why did God punish them with death?

_____

_____

_____

Q 6.   (Acts 6) Who did the multitude of disciples appoint to look after the widows, and what did they call upon the apostles to do?

_____

_____

_____

Q 7.   (Acts 7) What did Stephen see just before his oppressors stoned him to death?

_____

_____

_____

Q 8.   (Acts 8) Who baptized the Ethiopian eunuch, and what happened to Philip immediately afterward?

_____

_____

Q 9.   (Acts 9) When the Jews planned to kill Saul (Paul), who helped him escape to Jerusalem?

_____

_____

_____

Q 10.   (Acts 10) What did an angel of the Lord tell Cornelius to do, and where did Simon Peter live?

_____

_____

_____

Q 11.   (Acts 11) How long did Barnabas and Saul (Paul) assemble at the church at Antioch, and what did they do there?

_____

_____

_____

Q 12.   (Acts 12) How did Herod die?

_____

_____

_____

Q 13.   (Acts 13) What happened when Saul (Paul) told the sorcerer, Elymas, that he would be blind for a season for trying to prevent the deputy, Sergius Paulus, from hearing God's Word?

_____

_____

_____

Q 14.   (Acts 14) Who did Paul heal at Lystra?

_____

_____

_____

Q 15.   (Acts 15) What caused Paul and Barnabas to separate, and where did they go?

_____

_____

_____

Q 16.   (Acts 16) What was Lydia's occupation?

_____

_____

_____

Q 17.   (Acts 17) At Thessalonica, whose house did the Jews attack?

_____

_____

_____

Q 18.   (Acts 18) Which couple did Paul live with at Corinth, and what were their occupations?

_____

_____

_____

Q 19.   (Acts 19) What caused the riot at Ephesus?

_____

_____

_____

Q 20.   (Acts 20) One day, while Paul preached, what happened to
         Eutychus?

_____

_____

_____

Q 21.   (Acts 21) Who demanded to know Paul's identity during his arrest?

_____

_____

_____

Q 22.   (Acts 22) Who surrounded Paul (Saul) on his journey to Damascus?

_____

_____

_____

Q 23.   (Acts 23) How many Jews made a conspiracy against Paul?

_____

_____

_____

Q 24.   (Acts 24) Who was Ananias, and who did he bring with him to
         accuse Paul?

_____

_____

_____

Q 25.   (Acts 25) After the Jews made many accusations against Paul,
         Festus asked Paul if he would rather go to Jerusalem for his trial,
         and Paul requested to appeal to Caesar. Where did Festus send Paul?

_____

_____

_____

Q 26.   (Acts 26) At Paul's trial before King Agrippa, what did the king tell
         Paul he was permitted to do?

_____

_____

_____

Q 27. (Acts 27) What was the name of the wind that struck the ship that could not withstand the storm?

_____

_____

_____

Q 28. (Acts 28) How long did Paul spend at the house he hired, and what did he do?

_____

_____

_____

Score: **/28 points**

Reflection and Prayer-The Book of Acts

Reflect on Chapters 1-28, and choose one verse that speaks to your heart. Write the verse.

Prayer: Write a prayer asking God to help you apply the verse to situations in your own life.

Read **The Book of Romans** *before continuing.*

Questions - The Book of Romans

Q 1.   (Romans 1) Why is Paul eager to see the Romans?

_____

_____

_____

Q 2.   (Romans 2) What happens to those who judge others?

_____

_____

_____

Q 3.   (Romans 3) How are sinners justified?

_____

_____

_____

Q 4.   (Romans 4) Which characters from the Scriptures does Paul refer to when speaking of righteousness?

_____

_____

_____

Q 5.   (Romans 5) How do we obtain peace with God?

_____

_____

_____

Q 6.   (Romans 6) Believers are dead to what?

_____

_____

_____

Q 7.   (Romans 7) According to the Law, what binds a woman to her husband?

_____

_____

_____

Q 8.   (Romans 8) According to Paul's teaching on life in the Spirit, who are the sons of God?

_____

_____

_____

Q 9.   (Romans 9) Who said God would save a remnant of Israel?

_____

_____

_____

Q 10.   (Romans 10) According to Paul, which righteousness did Moses describe?

_____

_____

_____

Q 11.   (Romans 11) How does Paul describe his heritage?

_____

_____

_____

Q 12.   (Romans 12) How does Paul tell the Romans to treat persecutors?

_____

_____

_____

Q 13.   (Romans 13) What does Paul say about resisting the authority of higher powers?

_____

_____

_____

Q 14.   (Romans 14) Which things does Paul say we should seek?

_____

_____

_____

Q 15.   (Romans 15) What is Paul's reason for writing to the Romans?

_____

_____

_____

Q 16.   (Romans 16) Who does Paul commend unto the Romans, and what
is his accolade for this person?

_____

_____

_____

Score: /16 points

Reflection and Prayer-The Book of Romans

Reflect on Chapters 1-16, and choose one verse that speaks
to your heart. Write the verse.

*Prayer: Write a prayer asking God to help you apply
the verse to situations in your own life.*

*Read **The Book of I Corinthians** before continuing.*

Questions - The Book of 1 Corinthians

Q 1.   (1 Corinthians 1) What caused Paul to implore those at Corinth to put aside contentions and join together?

_____

_____

_____

Q 2.   (1 Corinthians 2) How does God reveal the deep things of God to those who love Him?

_____

_____

_____

Q 3.   (1 Corinthians 3) What example does Paul give of labouring together with God?

_____

_____

_____

Q 4.   (1 Corinthians 4) How does Paul regard Timotheus (Timothy)?

_____

_____

_____

Q 5.   (1 Corinthians 5) Who does Paul identify as immoral?

_____

_____

_____

Q 6.   (1 Corinthians 6) What question does Paul raise regarding lawsuits
         among believers?

_____

_____

_____

Q 7.   (1 Corinthians 7) Should a woman or man leave an unbelieving
         spouse?

_____

_____

_____

Q 8.   (1 Corinthians 8) What is Paul teaching about offering food to idols?

_____

_____

_____

Q 9.   (1 Corinthians 9) What is the seal of Paul's apostleship?

_____

_____

_____

Q 10.   (1 Corinthians 10) What does Paul teach about temptation?

_____

_____

_____

Q 11.   (1 Corinthians 11) According to Paul, how should a woman pray and
         prophesize?

_____

_____

_____

Q 12.   (1 Corinthians 12) What does Paul say about spiritual gifts?

_____

_____

_____

Q 13.   (1 Corinthians 13) What will never fail?

_____

_____

_____

Q 14.   (1 Corinthians 14) What does Paul say about "speaking in tongues"
           and prophesying?

_____

_____

_____

Q 15.   (1 Corinthians 15) Who first saw Jesus after the resurrection?

_____

_____

_____

Q 16.   (1 Corinthians 16) What instructions does Paul give the church
           of Galatia and Corinth at the end of the epistle?

_____

_____

_____

Score: /16 points

Reflection and Prayer-The Book of 1 Corinthians

Reflect on Chapters 1-16, and choose one verse that speaks
to your heart. Write the verse.

*Prayer: Write a prayer asking God to help you apply
the verse to situations in your own life.*

*Read **The Book of 2 Corinthians** before continuing.*

Questions - The Book of 2 Corinthians

Q 1.   (2 Corinthians 1) How does Paul explain God's comfort?

_____

_____

_____

Q 2.   (2 Corinthians 2) How should the church respond to those who have caused grief or offense?

_____

_____

_____

Q 3.   (2 Corinthians 3) What does Paul say about God's sufficiency?

_____

_____

_____

Q 4.   (2 Corinthians 4) What happens to the minds of those who do not believe in Christ?

_____

_____

_____

Q 5.   (2 Corinthians 5) Paul discusses the concept of judgment. What will happen to every believer at the judgment seat of Christ?

_____

_____

_____

Q 6.   (2 Corinthians 6) How does Paul describe believers in verse 16?

_____

_____

_____

Q 7.   (2 Corinthians 7) How did Paul receive good news in Macedonia?

_____

_____

_____

Q 8.   (2 Corinthians 8) How does Paul describe Titus' ministry?

_____

_____

_____

Q 9.   (2 Corinthians 9) What kind of giver does God love?

_____

_____

_____

Q 10.   (2 Corinthians 10) What does Paul say about our weapons?

_____

_____

_____

Q 11.   (2 Corinthians 11) How many shipwrecks did Paul survive?

_____

_____

_____

Q 12.   (2 Corinthians 12) What is Paul's appeal to the Corinthians?

_____

_____

_____

Q 13.   (2 Corinthians 13) What command does Paul make to the
            Corinthians when ending the epistle?

_____

_____

_____

Score: /13 points

Reflection and Prayer-The Book of 2 Corinthians

Reflect on Chapters 1-13, and choose one verse that speaks
to your heart. Write the verse.

*Prayer: Write a prayer asking God to help you apply
the verse to situations in your own life.*

*Read **The Book of Galatians** before continuing.*

Questions - The Book of Galatians

Q 1.   (Galatians 1) Paul certifies that he did not receive the Gospel he preached from man or through man's teaching. How did Paul receive the Gospel?

_____

_____

_____

Q 2.   (Galatians 2) What evidence does Paul give that the church accepted him?

_____

_____

_____

Q 3.   (Galatians 3) Who does Paul say could also receive the blessing Abraham received from God?

_____

_____

_____

Q 4.   (Galatians 4) What did Paul tell the Galatians about freedom from bondage?

_____

_____

_____

Q 5.   (Galatians 5) Which warning does Paul give the Galatians?

_____

_____

_____

Q 6.   (Galatians 6) Where was Paul when he wrote to the Galatians?

_____

_____

_____

Score: /6 points

Reflection and Prayer-The Book of Galatians

Reflect on Chapters 1-6, and choose one verse that speaks to
your heart. Write the verse.

*Prayer: Write a prayer asking God to help you apply
the verse to situations in your own life.*

*Read **The Book of Ephesians** before continuing.*

Questions - The Book of Ephesians

Q 1.   (Ephesians 1) What had Paul heard about the Ephesians?

_____

_____

_____

Q 2.   (Ephesians 2) How does God quicken us?

_____

_____

_____

Q 3.   (Ephesians 3) How does Paul describe the gift of God's grace he
        received?

_____

_____

_____

Q 4.   (Ephesians 4) According to Paul, who walks in vanity?

_____

_____

_____

Q 5.   (Ephesians 5) How does Paul say men should love their wives?

_____

_____

_____

Q 6.   (Ephesians 6) What command does Paul give children, and what
        does he say will be the result of following this command?

_____

_____

_____

Score: /6 points

Reflection and Prayer-The Book of Ephesians

Reflect on Chapters 1-6, and choose one verse that speaks to
your heart. Write the verse.

*Prayer: Write a prayer asking God to help you apply
the verse to situations in your own life.*

*Read **The Book of Philippians** before continuing.*

Questions - The Book of Philippians

Q 1.   (Philippians 1) With Timotheus (Timothy), who does Paul address at Philippi, and what does he desire?

_____

_____

_____

Q 2.   (Philippians 2) How does Paul tell the Philippians to live in a corrupt society?

_____

_____

_____

Q 3.   (Philippians 3) Finish this verse: "I press toward the mark" (Philippians 3:14 KJV).

_____

_____

_____

Q 4.   (Philippians 4) What does Paul communicate to the Philippians
        about their gift-giving toward his ministry?

_____

_____
_____

Score: /4 points

Reflection and Prayer-The Book of Philippians

Reflect on Chapters 1-4, and choose one verse that speaks to
your heart. Write the verse.

*Prayer: Write a prayer asking God to help you apply
the verse to situations in your own life.*

*Read **The Book of Colossians** before continuing.*

Questions - The Book of Colossians

Q 1.   (Colossians 1) How does Paul's prayer for the Colossians begin and
         end?

_____

_____

_____

Q 2.   (Colossians 2) How does Paul describe the sufficiency of Christ?

_____

_____

_____

Q 3.   (Colossians 3) What does Paul tell the Colossians to avoid?

_____

_____

_____

Q 4.   (Colossians 4) In Paul's final words to the Colossians, what request does he make regarding the epistles?

_____

_____

_____

Score: /4 points

Reflection and Prayer-The Book of Colossians

Reflect on Chapters 1-4, and choose one verse that speaks to your heart. Write the verse.

Prayer: Write a prayer asking God to help you apply the verse to situations in your own life.

*Read **The Book of I Thessalonians** before continuing.*

Questions - The Book of 1 Thessalonians

Q 1.   (1 Thessalonians 1) Where did the Thessalonians spread the Lord's Word?

_____

_____

_____

Q 2.   (1 Thessalonians 2) Which words did Paul not use while carrying out God's work in Thessalonica?

_____

_____

_____

Q 3.   (1 Thessalonians 3) Why did Paul send Timotheus (Timothy) to Thessalonica?

_____

_____

_____

Q 4.   (1 Thessalonians 4) When the Lord descends, what will happen to the dead who are in Christ, and what will happen afterward?

_____

_____

_____

Q 5.   (1 Thessalonians 5) Where was Paul when he wrote 1
        Thessalonians?

_____

_____

_____

Score: /5 points

Reflection and Prayer-The Book of 1 Thessalonians

Reflect on Chapters 1-5, and choose one verse that speaks to
    your heart. Write the verse.

*Prayer: Write a prayer asking God to help you apply
    the verse to situations in your own life.*

*Read **The Book of 2 Thessalonians** before continuing.*

Questions - The Book of 2 Thessalonians

Q 1.   (2 Thessalonians 1) What does Paul say will happen to those who do
        not know God or obey Christ's Gospel?

_____

_____

_____

Q 2.   (2 Thessalonians 2) How does Paul feel toward the Thessalonians?

_____

_____

_____

Q 3.   (2 Thessalonians 3) What command does Paul make about
        associating with the disorderly?

_____

_____

_____

Score: /3 points

Reflection and Prayer-The Book of 2 Thessalonians

Reflect on Chapters 1-3, and choose one verse
that speaks to your heart. Write the verse.

*Prayer: Write a prayer asking God to help you
apply the verse to situations in your own life.*

Read **The Book of I Timothy** before continuing.

Questions - The Book of 1 Timothy

Q 1.   (1 Timothy 1) When Paul went to Macedonia, why did he tell
        Timothy to stay at Ephesus?

_____

_____

_____

Q 2.   (1 Timothy 2) What does Paul exhort as a pattern for prayer?

_____

_____

_____

Q 3.   (1 Timothy 3) How should a bishop rule his home?

_____

_____

_____

Q 4.   (1 Timothy 4) What does Paul tell Timothy to do as a leader until he
        visits?

_____

_____

_____

Q 5.   (1 Timothy 5) What does Paul say about the care of widows?

_____

_____

_____

Q 6.   (1 Timothy 6) What was the chief city of Phrygia?

_____

_____

_____

Score: /6 points

Reflection and Prayer-The Book of 1 Timothy

Reflect on Chapters 1-6, and choose one verse that speaks to
your heart. Write the verse.

*Prayer: Write a prayer asking God to help you apply
the verse to situations in your own life.*

*Read **The Book of 2 Timothy** before continuing.*

Questions - The Book of 2 Timothy

Q 1.   (2 Timothy 1) When Paul encourages Timothy to remain faithful, whose faith does he recall?

_____

_____

_____

Q 2.   (2 Timothy 2) What does Paul tell Timothy about being a workman?

_____

_____

_____

Q 3.   (2 Timothy 3) What does Paul tell Timothy about the godliness that will exist during the last days?

_____

_____

_____

Q 4.   (2 Timothy 4) Where did Paul send Tychicus?

_____

_____

_____

Score: /4 points

Reflection and Prayer-The Book of 2 Timothy

Reflect on Chapters 1-4, and choose one verse that speaks to your heart. Write the verse.

Prayer: Write a prayer asking God to help you apply the verse to situations in your own life.

*Read **The Book of Titus** before continuing.*

Questions - The Book of Titus

Q 1.   (Titus 1) What was Titus' task in Crete?

_____

_____

_____

Q 2.   (Titus 2) Who does Paul say should be sober-minded?

_____

_____

_____

Q 3.   (Titus 3) What should be the attitude toward heretics, according to
        Paul?

_____

_____

_____

Score: /3 points

*Read **The Book of Philemon** before continuing.*

Questions - The Book of Philemon

Q 1.   (Philemon) What is Paul's appeal to Philemon about his former
servant, Onesimus, who wronged him?

_____
_____
_____

Score: /1 point

Reflection and Prayer-The Books
of Titus and Philemon
Reflect on the books of Titus and Philemon, and choose one verse
that speaks to your heart. Write the verse.
*Prayer: Write a prayer asking God to help you apply
the verse to situations in your own life.*

*Read **The Book of Hebrews** before continuing.*

Questions - The Book of Hebrews

Q 1.   (Hebrews 1) How did God speak in times past, and how did He speak in later times?

_____

_____

_____

Q 2.   (Hebrews 2) According to Hebrews 2:18, what is one reason Jesus suffered temptation?

_____

_____

_____

Q 3.   (Hebrews 3) According to the author of Hebrews, what kept some from entering into Christ's rest?

_____

_____

_____

Q 4.   (Hebrews 4) How does Christ provide a way to God?

_____

_____

_____

Q 5.   (Hebrews 5) Who was Melchisedek (Melchizedek)?

_____

_____

_____

Q 6.   (Hebrews 6) According to the author of Hebrews, who received the promise of God?

_____

_____

_____

Q 7.   (Hebrews 7) What did Abraham give Melchisedek (Melchizedek)?

_____

_____

_____

Q 8.   (Hebrews 8) Where is our high priest?

_____

_____

_____

Q 9.   (Hebrews 9) How does the author describe Christ's sacrifice?

_____

_____

_____

Q 10.   (Hebrews 10) What does the author say about the daily sacrifices the priests offer?

_____

_____

_____

Q 11.   (Hebrews 11) Who are the first three examples of faith discussed in Hebrews 11?

_____

_____

_____

Q 12.   (Hebrews 12) Where is Mount Sion (Zion)?

_____

_____

_____

Q 13.   (Hebrews 13) Why is it essential to entertain strangers?

_____

_____

_____

Score: /13 points

Reflection and Prayer-The Book of Hebrews

Reflect on Chapters 1-13, and choose one verse that speaks
to your heart. Write the verse.

*Prayer: Write a prayer asking God to help you apply
the verse to situations in your own life.*

*Read **The Book of James** before continuing.*

Questions - The Book of James

Q 1.   (James 1) Who deceives themselves, according to James?

_____

_____

_____

Q 2.   (James 2) Who does James point to as examples of those justified by faith?

_____

_____

_____

Q 3.   (James 3) The tongue is full of what, according to James?

_____

_____

_____

Q 4.   (James 4) What does James say happens when we draw close to God?

_____

_____

_____

Q 5.   (James 5) What happened when Elias (Elijah) prayed that it would not rain, and what happened when he prayed again? Who does Elias (Elijah) represent to James?

_____

_____

_____

Score: /5 points

Reflection and Prayer-The Book of James

Reflect on Chapters 1-5, and choose one verse that speaks to your heart. Write the verse.

Prayer: Write a prayer asking God to help you apply the verse to situations in your own life.

*Read **The Book of I Peter** before continuing.*

Questions - The Book of 1 Peter

Q 1.   (1 Peter 1) Which similes does Peter use to describe flesh?

_____

_____

_____

Q 2.   (1 Peter 2) How does Peter describe Christ?

_____

_____

_____

Q 3.   (1 Peter 3) According to 1 Peter 3:8, what traits should Christians display?

_____

_____

_____

Q 4.   (1 Peter 4) What does Peter say about showing hospitality?

_____

_____

_____

Q 5.   (1 Peter 5) What does Peter say we should do with our cares?

_____

_____

_____

Score: /5 points

Reflection and Prayer-The Book of 1 Peter

Reflect on Chapters 1-5, and choose one verse that speaks to
your heart. Write the verse.

*Prayer: Write a prayer asking God to help you apply
the verse to situations in your own life.*

*Read **The Book of 2 Peter** before continuing.*

Questions - The Book of 2 Peter

Q 1.   (2 Peter 1) How did prophecy arise, according to Peter?

_____

_____

_____

Q 2.   (2 Peter 2) Whose ass (donkey) spoke?

_____

_____

_____

Q 3.   (2 Peter 3) How does Peter describe Christ's return?

_____

_____

_____

Score: **/3 points**

Reflection and Prayer--The Book of 2 Peter

Reflect on Chapters 1-3, and choose one verse that speaks to
your heart. Write the verse.

*Prayer: Write a prayer asking God to help you apply
the verse to situations in your own life.*

*Read **The Book of I John** before continuing.*

Questions - The Book of 1 John

Q 1.   (1 John 1) According to John, what happens when we say we do not sin?

_____

_____

_____

Q 2.   (1 John 2) Who lives in the light, according to John?

_____

_____

_____

Q 3.   (1 John 3) Which commandments of Christ does John speak about at the end of this chapter?

_____

_____

_____

Q 4.   (1 John 4) What is a man who says he loves God but hates his brother?

_____

_____

_____

Q 5.   (1 John 5) At the end of the epistle, what warning does John give his audience?

_____

_____

_____

Score: /5 points

Reflection and Prayer-The Book of 1 John

Reflect on Chapters 1-5, and choose one verse that speaks to your heart. Write the verse.

Prayer: Write a prayer asking God to help you apply the verse to situations in your own life.

*Read **The Book of 2 John** before continuing.*

Questions - The Book of 2 John

Question

Q 1.   (2 John) In this chapter, what is the meaning of love?

_____
_____
_____

Score: /1 point

*Read **The Book of 3 John** before continuing.*

Questions - The Book of 3 John

Question

Q 1.   (3 John) Who does John address?

_____

_____

_____

Score: /1 point

*Read **The Book of Jude** before continuing.*

Questions - The Book of Jude

Q 1.   (Jude) What appeal does Jude make in verse 3?

_____

_____
_____

Score: /1 point

Reflection and Prayer – The Books of 2 John, 3 John, and Jude

Reflect on the books of 2 John, 3 John, and Jude, and choose one verse that speaks to your heart. Write the verse.

Prayer: Write a prayer asking God to help you apply the verse to situations in your own life.

*Read **The Book of Revelation** before continuing.*

Questions - The Book of Revelation

Q 1.   (Revelation 1) Jesus is the source of the revelation John received for the seven churches. How did the revelation come to John?

_____

_____

_____

Q 2.   (Revelation 2) Why did John's message tell the church at Ephesus to repent?

_____

_____

_____

Q 3.   (Revelation 3) What was the problem with the church at Laodicea?

_____

_____

_____

Q 4.   (Revelation 4) What did John see surrounding the Throne in Heaven?

_____

_____

_____

Q 5.   (Revelation 5) John saw the Son of Man sitting on a Throne holding a book. An angel asked who was worthy to open the book. Which men could open the book?

_____

_____

_____

Q 6.   (Revelation 6) When John saw the Lamb opening the sixth seal, an earthquake took place, the sun turned black, and the moon looked like blood. What happened to the stars?

_____

_____

_____

Q 7.   (Revelation 7) How many of God's servants did the angels seal?

_____

_____

_____

Q 8.   (Revelation 8) What happened when John saw the Lamb opening the seventh seal?

_____

_____

_____

Q 9.   (Revelation 9) Who received the key of "the bottomless pit"?

_____

_____

_____

Q 10.   (Revelation 10) What happened when John asked the angel for the little book?

_____

_____

_____

Q 11.   (Revelation 11) How did John describe the reed?

_____

_____

_____

Q 12.   (Revelation 12) Who fought the dragon during the war in Heaven?

_____

_____

_____

Q 13.   (Revelation 13) What restrictions did the beast place on those who did not receive the mark?

_____

_____

_____

Q 14.   (Revelation 14) Who did John see standing on Mount Sion (Zion), and who was with Him? What appeared on their foreheads?

_____

_____

_____

Q 15.   (Revelation 15) What did one of the beasts give the seven angels?

_____

_____

_____

Q 16.   (Revelation 16) What happened to the islands and mountains in Revelation 16:20?

_____

_____

_____

Q 17.   (Revelation 17) When the Spirit took John to the wilderness, what did John see?

_____

_____

Q 18.   (Revelation 18) John saw an angel who told him that the city of Babylon had fallen. How long did it take for the city to fall?

_____

_____

_____

Q 19.   (Revelation 19) What happened to the beast in Revelation 19:20?

_____

_____

_____

Q 20.   (Revelation 20) What did the angel coming from Heaven have in his
         hand?

_____

_____

_____

Q 21.   (Revelation 21) To whom does John compare Jerusalem?

_____

_____

_____

Q 22.   (Revelation 22) What does John say will happen to those who add to
         his prophecy?

_____

_____

_____

Score: **/22 points**

Reflection and Prayer - The Book of Revelation

Reflect on Chapters 1-22, and choose one verse that speaks to your
heart. Write the verse.

Prayer: Write a prayer asking God to help you apply
the verse to situations in your own life.

Final score

Book of Matthew	/28	Book of 2 Thessalonians	/3
Book of Mark	/16	Book of I Timothy	/6
Book of Luke	/24	Book of 2 Timothy	/4
Book of John	/21	Book of Titus	/3
Book of Acts	/28	Book of Philemon	/1
Book of Romans	/16	Book of Hebrews	/13
Book of I Corinthians	/16	The Book of James	/5
Book of 2 Corinthians	/13	Book of I Peter	/5
Book of Galatians	/6	Book of 2 Peter	/3
Book of Ephesians	/6	Book of I John	/5
Book of Philippians	/4	Book of 2 John	/1
Book of Colossians	/4	Book of 3 John	/1
Book of I Thessalonians	/5	Book of Jude	/1
		Book of Revelation	/22

Total Score: /260

ANSWERS

Complete all the quizzes before continuing..

Questions and Answers - The Book of Matthew

Q 1.   (Matthew 1) What is the interpretation of the name Emmanuel?

A 1.   *Emmanuel means "God with us" (King James Version (KJV), Matthew 1:23).*

Q 2.   (Matthew 2) Which king ruled at the time of Jesus' birth in Bethlehem, and why did he assemble the chief priests and scribes?

A 2.   *Herod felt troubled when Wise Men from the east arrived to see Jesus, and he demanded to know where Christ would be born (Matthew 2:3-4 KJV).*

Q 3.   (Matthew 3) Where did John the Baptist preach, and which prophet foretold John's ministry?

A 3.   *John preached in the wilderness. The prophet Esaias (Isaiah) spoke of John's preaching, saying, "The voice of one crying in the wilderness, Prepare ye the way of the Lord, make his paths straight" (Matthew 3:1, 3 KJV).*

Q 4.   (Matthew 4) By the Sea of Galilee, which men did Jesus call to follow Him, and what were they doing?

A 4.   *Jesus first called Simon (called Peter) and Andrew as they cast a net. Then, Jesus called James and John; they were mending nets. Immediately, they all followed Jesus (Matthew 4:18-22 KJV).*

Q 5.   (Matthew 5) Seeing a multitude of people, Jesus ascended a mountain. When he sat down, the disciples joined him. What did Jesus do next?

A 5.   *Jesus started teaching His disciples about the blessings of those who follow Him. These teachings are called the Beatitudes (Matthew 5:1-11 KJV).*

Q 6.   (Matthew 6) What did Jesus teach about treasures on earth and in Heaven?

A 6.   *Jesus taught the futility of valuing earthly possessions and the importance of placing treasures in Heaven: "Lay not up for yourselves treasures on earth, where moth and rust doth corrupt, and where thieves break through and steal: / But lay up for yourselves treasures in heaven, where neither moth nor rust doth corrupt, and where thieves do not break through nor steal": (Matthew 6:19-20 KJV).*

Q 7.   (Matthew 7) Jesus told several parables in Matthew Chapter 7. After Jesus spoke these parables, what astonished the people about His teachings?

A 7.   *Unlike the scribes, Jesus taught with authority; Jesus' teachings astonished them (Matthew 7:28-29 KJV).*

Q 8.   (Matthew 8) Why did the centurion seek Jesus, and how did Jesus respond?

A 8.   *The centurion sought Jesus because his servant was sick; Jesus said He would heal the servant. Jesus marvelled at the centurion's faith, sent him on his way, and healed his servant (Matthew 8:5-13 KJV).*

Q 9.   (Matthew 9) Who touched the hem of Jesus' garment?

A 9.   *A woman sick for twelve years touched Jesus' hem, believing she would receive healing. Jesus observed the woman's faith and healed the woman (Matthew 9:20-22 KJV).*

Q 10.   (Matthew 10) How many disciples did Jesus call?

A 10.   Jesus called twelve disciples: Simon (Peter), Andrew, James and John (Zebedee's sons), Philip, Bartholomew, Thomas, Matthew, James (Alphaeus' son), Lebbaeus, Simon (the Canaanite), and Judas Iscariot. Jesus gave His disciples power to cast out unclean spirits and heal diseases (Matthew 10:1-4 KJV).

Q 11.   (Matthew 11) While in prison, what did John the Baptist do upon hearing of Christ's works and preaching in the cities?

A 11.   John sent two of his disciples who asked Christ, "Art thou he that should come, or do we look for another?" (Matthew 11:1-3 KJV).

Q 12.   (Matthew 12) Jesus went into the synagogue and encountered a man with a withered hand. After telling the man to stretch out his hand, Jesus restored the man's hand. What did the Pharisees do?

A 12.   The Pharisees left and made plans to destroy Jesus (Matthew 12:9-14 KJV).

Q 13.   (Matthew 13) In the parable of the sower, what happened to the seeds that fell on good ground?

A 13.   In the parable, the seeds produced fruit. Jesus pointed out that the seeds represent those who hear the Word, understand it, and produce good fruit in their lives (Matthew 13:8, 23 KJV).

Q 14.   (Matthew 14) How did John the Baptist die, and what did his disciples do with his body?

A 14.   Herod had John beheaded. John's disciples buried his body and told Jesus about John's death (Matthew 14:9-12 KJV).

Q 15.   (Matthew 15) Jesus performed a miracle and fed a multitude of four thousand who had not eaten in three days. What did Jesus feed the multitude, and what was left?

A 15.   *First, Jesus asked His disciples how many loaves of bread they had, and they told Him seven loaves and a few fish. Then, Jesus took the seven loaves and the fish, gave thanks, and handed it to the disciples to feed the multitude. After the multitude had eaten, seven baskets remained (Matthew 15:34-38 KJV).*

Q 16.   (Matthew 16) To tempt Jesus, what did the Pharisees and Sadducees ask Him to show them, and what did He tell them about seeking a sign?

A 16.   *The Pharisees and Sadducees asked for "a sign from heaven." Jesus told them they were a "worthless and adulterous generation" for seeking a sign, and the only sign would be that of Jonas (Jonah), the prophet; then Jesus left (Matthew 16:1, 4 KJV).*

Q 17.   (Matthew 17) Who did Jesus take to His transfiguration, and where did they go?

A 17.   *Jesus took Peter, James, and John to ascend a "high mountain" (Matthew 17:1-2 KJV).*

Q 18.   (Matthew 18) How did Jesus respond when the disciples asked, "Who is the greatest in the kingdom of heaven" (Matthew 18:1 KJV)?

A 18.   *Jesus placed a child amid the disciples and said, "Verily I say unto you, Except ye be converted, and become as little children, ye shall not enter into the kingdom of heaven" (Matthew 18:2-3 KJV).*

Q 19.   (Matthew 19) What did the young man seek when he came to Jesus, and why did Jesus' response cause the young man to feel sorrow?

A 19. *The young man asked Jesus what he could do to obtain eternal life; Jesus told him if he would sell his possessions and give to those in need, he would have treasures in Heaven; then Jesus told the young man to follow Him. The young man felt sorrow because he had many possessions and wanted to keep them (Matthew 19:16, 21-22 KJV).*

Q 20. (Matthew 20) In the parable of the labourers in the vineyard, how much did the householder agree to pay the labourers?

A 20. *The householder agreed to pay a penny each day (Matthew 20:2 KJV).*

Q 21. (Matthew 21) As Jesus came to the fig tree, what did He find, and what eventually happened to the tree?

A 21. *The fig tree contained nothing but leaves; immediately, it withered after Jesus conveyed it would never grow fruit (Matthew 21:19 KJV).*

Q 22. (Matthew 22) To deceive Jesus, what did the Pharisees ask, and how did they react to His response?

A 22. *The Pharisees asked if it were lawful to pay tribute to Caesar. Sensing their evil intentions to entangle Him, Jesus called them hypocrites and asked why they tempted Him. Finally, Jesus told them, "Render therefore unto Caesar the things which are Caesar's; and unto God the things that are God's." In awe, the Pharisees left (Matthew 22:17-23 KJV).*

Q 23. (Matthew 23) Jesus condemned the works of the Pharisees. What did Jesus say about their works and outward appearances?

A 23. *Jesus said the Pharisees tried to impress others by wearing their religious clothing in a showy way (Matthew 23:5 KJV).*

Q 24.   (Matthew 24) At the Mount of Olives, what did the disciples ask Jesus? How did Jesus answer the disciples' question?

A 24.   *The disciples asked which signs would signal Jesus' coming during end times; Jesus replied, "Take heed that no man deceive you. /For many shall come in my name, saying, I am Christ: and shall deceive many" (Matthew 24:3-5 KJV).*

Q 25.   (Matthew 25) Jesus told a parable of ten virgins. How did five virgins behave wisely, and how did five behave foolishly on their way to meet the bridegroom?

A 25.   *Five wise virgins took oil for their lamps, and five foolish ones did not (Matthew 25:3-4 KJV).*

Q 26.   (Matthew 26) What did a woman pour on Jesus' head at Simon the leper's home in Bethany?

A 26.   *The woman poured very precious ointment on Jesus' head, and Jesus recognized that the oil was for His burial (Matthew 26:7, 12 KJV).*

Q 27.   (Matthew 27) Who was Joseph of Arimathaea, and what did Joseph do after he begged Jesus' body?

A 27.   *Joseph of Arimathaea was a rich man and Jesus' disciple; he wrapped Jesus' body in linen cloth and laid it in his own tomb before rolling a large stone to the entrance of the sepulcher (Matthew 27:57-60 KJV).*

Q 28.   (Matthew 28) What time did Mary Magdalene and Mary go to the sepulcher, and what did the angel of the Lord tell the women?

A 28.   At dawn, Mary Magdalene and Mary went to the sepulcher, and the angel of the Lord told them Jesus had risen (Matthew 28:1-2, 6 KJV).

_____

Score   /28 points

Questions and Answers - The Book of Mark

Q 1.   (Mark 1) Who did John baptize in the wilderness?

A 1.   John baptized people from Judaea and Jerusalem in the river Jordan (Mark 1:4-5 KJV).

Q 2.   (Mark 2) Who was Levi's father, and where did Jesus see Levi and invite him to follow Him?

A 2.   Levi's father was Alphaeus; Jesus saw Levi at the receipt of custom and invited him to follow Him. Immediately, Levi followed Jesus (Mark 2:14 KJV).

Q 3.   (Mark 3) What did Jesus surname Simon?

A 3.   Jesus surnamed him Peter (Mark 3:16 KJV).

Q 4.   (Mark 4) In the parable of the sower, what happened to the seeds that fell into the thorns?

A 4.   The thorns "choked" the seeds, so they did not yield fruit; Jesus explained that the seeds represent those who hear the Word but allow worldly cares, possessions, and other things to keep their lives from being fruitful (Mark 4:7, 19 KJV).

Q 5.   (Mark 5) Jesus healed a man who had an unclean spirit then permitted the unclean spirits to enter a herd of swine that ran into the ocean and drowned. What was the man like afterward?

A 5.   The man was "in his right mind" (Mark 5:15 KJV).

Q 6. (Mark 6) What happened when Jesus went to His own country and taught in the synagogue?

A 6. *Although Jesus' teaching in the synagogue astonished many in His own country, they did not accept Jesus' wisdom and were offended when He taught in the synagogue. Their lack of faith caused Jesus to wonder (Mark 6:1-3, 6 KJV).*

Q 7. (Mark 7) Jesus healed a deaf man who had a speech impediment. What did Jesus do that showed the man his healing came from God?

A 7. *The man could hear and speak when Jesus looked to Heaven and said, "EPHPHATHA," . . . "Be opened" (Mark 7:34-35 KJV).*

Q 8. (Mark 8) Which events did Jesus foretell of His suffering, and how did Peter respond?

A 8. *Jesus said He had to face a time of suffering in which the elders, chief priests, and scribes would reject and kill Him, but after three days, He would rise again. Peter rebuked Jesus, but Jesus rebuked him for loving things of men, not God (Mark 8:31-33 KJV).*

Q 9. (Mark 9) Was Peter present at Jesus' transfiguration?

A 9. *Yes. Peter was with Jesus, James, and John; they were by themselves (Mark 9:2 KJV).*

Q 10. (Mark 10) Who was Bartimaeus, and where was he when Jesus passed by?

A 10. *Bartimaeus was Timaeus' blind son who begged beside the highway. He called out to Jesus for healing when he saw Jesus passing by. Jesus commanded those present to call the blind man, and when Bartimaeus came, he asked Jesus to heal him. Immediately, Jesus healed Bartimaeus' blindness (Mark 10:46-52 KJV).*

Q 11.   (Mark 11) Whose tables and chairs did Jesus overthrow in the Temple?

A 11.   Jesus sent out those who were buying and selling; He overthrew the moneychangers' tables and the chairs of those selling doves (Mark 11:15 KJV).

Q 12.   (Mark 12) What was the value of two mites?

A 12.   Two mites made a farthing. A poor widow tossed two mites into the treasury, and Jesus acknowledged her gift as more significant than the gift of others who were rich as she had given all she had, even what she needed to survive (Mark 12:42-44 KJV).

Q 13.   (Mark 13) Finish this verse: "Heaven and earth shall pass away: _____" (Mark 13:31 KJV).

A 13.   "Heaven and earth shall pass away: /but my words shall not pass away" (Mark 13:31 KJV).

Q 14.   (Mark 14) Although the chief priests and scribes wanted to put Jesus to death, why did they not choose to put Him to death during the Passover and the Feast of Unleavened Bread?

A 14.   The chief priests and scribes thought the people would cause chaos (Mark 14:1-2 KJV).

Q 15.   (Mark 15) At Jesus' crucifixion, the soldiers impelled Simon to carry Jesus' cross. Who was Simon?

A 15.   Simon was Alexander and Rufus' father; he was a Cyrenian passing by during Jesus' crucifixion (Mark 15:21).

Q 16.   (Mark 16) What did the women bring to the sepulcher, and what did they find?

A 16.   *The women brought spices to anoint Jesus, but they found the stone had rolled away (Mark 16:1, 4 KJV).*

_____

Score   /16 points

Questions and Answers - The Book of Luke

Q 1.   (Luke 1) What happened after Zacharias wrote "His name is John" on a tablet (Luke 1:63)?

A 1.   An angel of the Lord appeared to Zacharias, telling him his wife, Elisabeth, would have a son named John. When Zacharias did not believe the angel's words, the angel said he would not be able to speak because of his disbelief, and when Zacharias came out of the Temple, he could not speak. However, Elisabeth had a son, and at the child's circumcision, Elisabeth declared that the child's name should be John. When Zacharias wrote "His name is John" on the tablet, fulfilling the angel's words, his mouth opened, and he spoke again, praising God (Luke 1:11-13, 18-22, 57-64 KJV).

Q 2.   (Luke 2) Who was Anna, and what did she do daily and nightly?

A 2.   Advanced in age, Anna was a prophetess and widow; she did not leave the Temple but fasted and prayed every day and night (Luke 2:36-37 KJV).

Q 3.   (Luke 3) Why did Herod place John the Baptist in prison; what were the names of Herod's brother and his wife?

A 3.   Herod married his brother Philip's wife, Herodias, and when John reprimanded Herod for marrying Herodias and his wickedness, Herod placed John in prison (Luke 3:19-20 KJV).

Q 4.   (Luke 4) How long did Jesus spend in the wilderness?

A 4.   For forty days, Jesus was in the wilderness, where the devil tried to tempt Him; Satan left when he could not tempt Jesus (Luke 4:1-2, 13 KJV).

Q 5. (Luke 5) Where was Levi when Jesus invited him to follow Him, and what did Levi do after following Jesus?

A 5. *Levi was at the receipt of custom when Jesus called him; after following Jesus, Levi held a feast at his house among the publicans and others (Luke 5:27-29 KJV).*

Q 6. (Luke 6) One day, Jesus chose twelve disciples. What did Jesus do before He chose the disciples, and what did He call them?

A 6. *Before choosing the disciples, Jesus spent the night on a mountain praying, and Jesus called them apostles (Luke 6:12-13 KJV).*

Q 7. (Luke 7) At Capernaum, why did a centurion send his elders to Jesus, and what did Jesus do?

A 7. *The centurion sought Jesus to heal his dying servant; Jesus went with the elders, marvelled at the centurion's faith, and made the servant whole (Luke 7:2-10 KJV).*

Q 8. (Luke 8) Why did Jairus fall at the feet of Jesus?

A 8. *Jairus' twelve-year-old daughter was dying, so he wanted Jesus to come to his house. Although those nearby assumed she was dead, Jesus took her hand, told her to get up, and she arose (Luke 8:41-42, 52-55 KJV).*

Q 9. (Luke 9) Describe Jesus' countenance at His transfiguration.

A 9. *While Jesus prayed, His countenance changed, and His white raiment glistened. Peter and others witnessed Jesus' glory at His transfiguration (Luke 9:29, 32 KJV).*

Q 10.   (Luke 10) Who was Martha's sister, and what did the sisters do when Jesus visited Martha's house?

A 10.   Mary was Martha's sister; Mary listened to Jesus' words while sitting at His feet, but Martha busied herself serving Jesus (Luke 10:38-40 KJV).

Q 11.   (Luke 11) Jesus cast out a dumb devil. What did the devil do?

A 11.   The dumb devil spoke, causing amazement among the people (Luke 11:14 KJV).

Q 12.   (Luke 12) Jesus told a parable of a rich fool. What message did Jesus reveal at the end of the parable?

A 12.   The man is a fool for keeping his treasures to himself as they do nothing for his soul or his relationship with God (Luke 12:20-21 KJV).

Q 13.   (Luke 13) What did the woman with a spirit of infirmity do when Jesus spoke healing words and laid hands on her?

A 13.   Instantly, the woman stood uprightly and glorified God (Luke 13:13 KJV).

Q 14.   (Luke 14) Where and when did Jesus encounter a man who had dropsy?

A 14.   Jesus was at the home of one of the chief Pharisees on the Sabbath day when He encountered the man who had dropsy. When Jesus asked the lawyers and Pharisees if it were lawful to heal on the Sabbath day, they did not reply. Then, Jesus healed the man (Luke 14:1-4 KJV).

Q 15.   (Luke 15) In the parable of the lost sheep, how many sheep did the man have, and how many did he lose? How did the man respond upon finding the lost sheep?

A 15.   *The man had one hundred sheep; he lost one sheep and rejoiced when he found it. In this parable, Jesus illustrated that rejoicing also occurs in Heaven when one sinner repents (Luke 15:4-7 KJV).*

Q 16.   (Luke 16) Jesus told a parable about a rich man and his steward. What accusation did the rich man make toward his steward?

A 16.   *The rich man accused the steward of wasting his goods and demanded an account for the management of his resources, or he would lose his position as a steward (Luke 16:1-2 KJV).*

Q 17.   (Luke 17) How many lepers did Jesus heal on His way to Jerusalem?

A 17.   *In a village, ten lepers cried out to Jesus for mercy, and Jesus told them to show the priests. They obeyed Jesus and departed, cleansed of their leprosy as they left (Luke 17:12-14 KJV).*

Q 18.   (Luke 18) Jesus told a parable about a widow and a judge. What did the widow ask the judge, and how did the judge respond?

A 18.   *The woman asked the judge to avenge her of her adversary; at first, the judge refused but eventually avenged the woman so she would discontinue her requests. Afterward, Jesus showed the injustice of the judge by saying that God quickly avenges His own (Luke 18:3-8 KJV).*

Q 19.   (Luke 19) Who was Zacchaeus, and how did he get to see Jesus?

A 19.   *Zacchaeus was a small, wealthy man and chief of the publicans. One day, Zacchaeus climbed into a sycamore tree to see Jesus. Jesus told him to come down and take Him to his house. When Zacchaeus promised to give half of his possessions to the poor and repay fourfold anything he had acquired falsely, Jesus saved the household of Zacchaeus (Luke 19:2-9 KJV).*

Q 20.   (Luke 20) Who sent spies to deceive Jesus, and why?

A 20.   *The chief priests and scribes sent spies pretending to be good men to deceive Jesus so they could take Him to the governor and make accusations against Him. Jesus answered their deceptive questions about paying tribute to Caesar, saying, "Render therefore unto Caesar the things which be Caesar's, and unto God the things which be God's" (Luke 20:20-26 KJV).*

Q 21.   (Luke 21) Jesus taught in the Temple during the day. Where did He go at night?

A 21.   *At night, Jesus went to the Mount of Olives (Luke 21:37 KJV).*

Q 22.   (Luke 22) At Jesus' betrayal, what happened when one with Jesus struck the servant, cutting off his right ear?

A 22.   *Jesus touched the servant's ear and healed him (Luke 22:51 KJV).*

Q 23.   (Luke 23) What did Pilate do upon hearing that Jesus was a Galilaean, and where was Herod at the time?

A 23.   *Pilate sent Jesus to Herod at Jerusalem. Herod was pleased to see Jesus as he had heard about Him for a long time and hoped to witness one of Jesus' miracles (Luke 23:7-8 KJV).*

Q 24.   (Luke 24) What happened as two disciples walked toward Emmaus, and how far was it from Jerusalem?

A 24.   *While the disciples talked together about recent events, Jesus came near, but their eyes were "holden," so the disciples did not recognize Jesus. It was about threescore furlongs from Jerusalem (Luke 24:13-16 KJV).*

Score   /24 points

Questions and Answers - The Book of John

Q 1.   (John 1) The Pharisees asked John the Baptist why he baptized if he
were not Christ, Elias (Elijah), or the prophet. How did John show
humility toward Christ?

*A 1.   John said he baptized with water, but One greater would
come after him; then John added that he was not worthy of
unloosing the "latchet" of Christ's shoe (John 1:26-27 KJV).*

Q 2.   (John 2) At the marriage in Cana of Galilee, how many waterpots
needed filling?

*A 2.   There were six waterpots. Jesus performed His first miracle
by changing water into wine, showing His glory, and causing
His disciples to believe in Him (John 2:6-11 KJV).*

Q 3.   (John 3) How did Nicodemus know that God had sent Jesus to teach
and perform miracles?

*A 3.   Jesus' miracles showed His authority, so Nicodemus felt con-
fident that Jesus came from God (John 3:2 KJV).*

Q 4.   (John 4) What first influenced the Samaritans to believe in Christ,
and how long did Jesus remain with them?

*A 4.   At first, a woman's testimony influenced the Samaritans;
after Christ stayed with the Samaritans for two days, many
Samaritans heard His words and believed (John 4:39-43
KJV).*

Q 5.   (John 5) Where was the pool containing five porches, and what was the pool called?

A 5.   *The pool was in Jerusalem near the sheep market, and it was called Bethesda. Jesus healed an impotent man at the pool on the Sabbath day, and the man told the Jews that Jesus healed him (John 5:2, 5-9, 15 KJV).*

Q 6.   (John 6) How far had the disciples rowed before seeing Jesus walking on the sea, and how did they feel upon seeing Jesus?

A 6.   *The disciples had rowed approximately twenty-five or thirty furlongs; they were afraid upon seeing Jesus walking on water. Then Jesus told them not to be afraid and instantly moved the ship to shore (John 6:19-21 KJV).*

Q 7.   (John 7) Who came to see Jesus at night?

A 7.   *Nicodemus did (John 7:50 KJV).*

Q 8.   (John 8) The scribes and Pharisees brought a woman who had committed adultery to Jesus. What did they say?

A 8.   *The scribes and Pharisees said that according to the Law, the woman should be stoned. They tried to get Jesus to speak about it so they could condemn his answer (John 8:4-5 KJV).*

Q 9.   (John 9) The Pharisees asked the blind man how he received his sight. How did the blind man reply, and on which day did the blind man's healing occur?

A 9.   *The blind man told the Pharisees that Jesus made the clay and placed it on his eyes; when the blind man washed, he could see. Jesus performed this miracle on the Sabbath day (John 9:14-15 KJV).*

Q 10.   (John 10) What reason did the Jews give for wanting to stone Jesus?

A 10.   The Jews accused Jesus of blasphemy and claiming to be God (John 10:33 KJV).

Q 11.   (John 11) How long was Lazarus dead before Jesus raised him?

A 11.   Lazarus was dead for four days, but Jesus raised him, causing some Jews to believe in Christ (John 11:39, 43-45 KJV).

Q 12.   (John 12) The Greeks came to worship at a feast. What request did the Greeks make of Philip, and where was Philip's home?

A 12.   The Greeks requested to see Jesus; Philip was from Bethsaida of Galilee (John 12:21 KJV).

Q 13.   (John 13) Who did Jesus give the sop?

A 13.   Jesus said He would pass the sop to the one who would betray Him. He gave the sop to Judas Iscariot (John 13:26 KJV).

Q 14.   (John 14) Jesus told the disciples that knowing Him meant knowing the Father. Who asked Jesus to show them the Father?

A 14.   Philip asked Jesus to show them the Father. Jesus questioned Philip about his faith in Him (John 14:7-10 KJV).

Q 15.   (John 15) Jesus told His disciples he called them "friends," not servants. Why?

A 15.   Jesus told His disciples He called them "friends" because He shared with them what He heard from His Father. The disciples followed His commands, so He referred to them as friends (John 15:14-15 KJV).

Q 16.   (John 16) Who did Jesus say He would send when He went away?

A 16.   Jesus said He would send the Comforter. Jesus had to leave

for the Comforter to come (John 16:7 KJV).

Q 17.   (John 17) What was Jesus' prayer for His disciples?

A 17.   Jesus said the disciples were "not of the world" and prayed for their sanctification in the truth of Christ. Jesus sent the disciples into the world and prayed for them to be safe spiritually (John 17:14-19 KJV).

Q 18.   (John 18) How did Annas send Jesus to Caiaphas?

A 18.   Annas sent Jesus bound to Caiaphas (John 18:24 KJV).

Q 19.   (John 19) Who commanded the soldiers to scourge Jesus?

A 19.   Pilate gave the order for the soldiers to scourge Jesus. They placed a crown of thorns on His head, dressed Him in a purple robe, and smote Jesus (John 19:1-3 KJV).

Q 20.   (John 20) Which items did Simon Peter see in the sepulcher, and how were they arranged? What was the reaction of Peter and the other disciple that arrived?

A 20.   Peter saw the linen clothes and napkin; the napkin was by itself. Peter and the other disciple left, unaware of the Scripture that said Jesus would rise again (John 20:6-10 KJV).

Q 21.　(John 21) After Jesus' resurrection, where did He reveal Himself to the disciples?

A 21.　*After Jesus' resurrection, He revealed Himself at the Sea of Tiberias to Simon Peter, Thomas (Didymus), Nathanael, the sons of Zebedee, and two other disciples (John 21:1-2 KJV).*

———————————————————————————

Score　　**/21 points**

Questions and Answers - The Book of Acts

Q 1.   (Acts 1) How did the disciples choose Matthias to become an apostle?

A 1.   The apostles prayed first, asking God to direct their choice for an apostle; then they cast lots which fell on Matthias, and Matthias became an apostle (Acts 1:24-26 KJV).

Q 2.   (Acts 2) On the Day of Pentecost, what amazed the multitudes?

A 2.   The disciples spoke "with other tongues" that the multitudes heard in their own languages; the Holy Ghost filled them, making it possible for the apostles to speak in tongues (Acts 2:4, 6 KJV).

Q 3.   (Acts 3) What did the lame man at the gate called Beautiful do after Peter healed him?

A 3.   The lame man leaped up, walked, and went into the Temple, praising God; bystanders marvelled at the change in the man (Acts 3:8-10 KJV).

Q 4.   (Acts 4) Who was Joses (Joseph), and what did he do among the community of believers?

A 4.   Joses (Joseph) was a Levite surnamed Barnabas who sold his land and laid the money at the apostles' feet for distribution among the believers in need (Acts 4:35-37 KJV).

Q 5.   (Acts 5) Who were Ananias and Sapphira, and why did God punish them with death?

A 5. *Ananias and Sapphira, a married couple, sold land and placed a part of the price they received at the apostles' feet. Peter questioned Ananias about his actions and reminded him he had lied to God; then, Ananias fell dead. About three hours later, Peter asked Sapphira why she tempted God and told her Ananias had died and that she would die too. Sapphira fell dead at Peter's feet (Acts 5:1-10 KJV).*

Q 6. (Acts 6) Who did the multitude of disciples appoint to look after the widows, and what did they call upon the apostles to do?

A 6. *The multitude of disciples appointed Stephen, Philip, Prochorus, Nicanor, Timon, Parmenas, and Nicolas. The apostles prayed and laid hands on the men (Acts 6:5-6 KJV).*

Q 7. (Acts 7) What did Stephen see just before his oppressors stoned him to death?

A 7. *Stephen saw God's glory and Jesus standing at God's right hand (Acts 7:55 KJV).*

Q 8. (Acts 8) Who baptized the Ethiopian eunuch, and what happened to Philip immediately afterward?

A 8. *The Ethiopian eunuch asked Philip what prevented him from being baptized, so Philip asked him if he believed. When the eunuch answered that he believed Jesus was God's Son, Philip baptized him; the Lord's Spirit took Philip away, and the eunuch did not see Philip again (Acts 8:36-39 KJV).*

Q 9. (Acts 9) When the Jews planned to kill Saul (Paul), who helped him escape to Jerusalem?

A 9. *The disciples helped Saul (Paul) by bringing him down a wall in a basket at night (Acts 9:25 KJV).*

Q 10.   (Acts 10) What did an angel of the Lord tell Cornelius to do, and where did Simon Peter live?

A 10.   *In a vision, an angel of the Lord told Cornelius to go to Joppa to find Simon Peter, who would speak God's commands unto him; Simon Peter lived in the house of Simon, a tanner. Peter spoke God's truth to Cornelius (Acts 10:32-33 KJV).*

Q 11.   (Acts 11) How long did Barnabas and Saul (Paul) assemble at the church at Antioch, and what did they do there?

A 11.   *Barnabas and Saul stayed for a year and taught many people (Acts 11:26 KJV).*

Q 12.   (Acts 12) How did Herod die?

A 12.   *When Herod dressed royally and made a speech from the throne, people said he sounded like a god. Instantly, the angel of the Lord struck Herod as he had failed to give glory to God. Worms ate him, and he died (Acts 12:21-23 KJV).*

Q 13.   (Acts 13) What happened when Saul (Paul) told the sorcerer, Elymas, that he would be blind for a season for trying to prevent the deputy, Sergius Paulus, from hearing God's Word?

A 13.   *Paul (Saul) told Elymas the Lord would strike him blind and reminded him of his wickedness: "And now, behold, the hand of the Lord is upon thee, and thou shalt be blind, not seeing the sun for a season. And immediately there fell on him a mist and a darkness; and he went about seeking some to lead him by the hand" (Acts 13:11 KJV).*

Q 14.   (Acts 14) Who did Paul heal at Lystra?

A 14.   *Perceiving the man's faith, Paul shouted for a disabled man to get up and healed him. The man had the faith needed for healing, so he leaped and walked (Acts 14:8-10 KJV).*

Q 15.   (Acts 15) What caused Paul and Barnabas to separate, and where did they go?

A 15.   **Barnabas wanted to take John Mark with them, but Paul disagreed. So, Barnabas took Mark to Cyprus, and Paul took Silas through Syria and Cilicia (Acts 15:37-41 KJV).**

Q 16.   (Acts 16) What was Lydia's occupation?

A 16.   **Lydia sold purple at Thyatira (Acts 16:14 KJV).**

Q 17.   (Acts 17) At Thessalonica, whose house did the Jews attack?

A 17.   **The Jews attacked Jason's house. They were envious because Paul spent three Sabbath days preaching about Christ at the Jewish synagogue. Some Jews who heard Paul preach believed Paul's teachings about Christ, and many Greeks believed as well, causing envy among the Jews (Acts 17:1-5 KJV).**

Q 18.   (Acts 18) Which couple did Paul live with at Corinth, and what were their occupations?

A 18.   **Paul lived with Aquila and his wife Priscilla; they were tent-makers (Acts 18:1-3 KJV).**

Q 19.   (Acts 19) What caused the riot at Ephesus?

A 19.   **Demetrius, a silversmith, informed other artisans that their craft could end due to Paul's teachings against the gods they made with their hands. Also, he feared that the temple of Diana could face destruction. The riot caused a great deal of confusion, with many unaware of the cause of the event (Acts 19:24-29, 32 KJV).**

Q 20.   (Acts 20) One day, while Paul preached, what happened to Eutychus?

A 20.   **Eutychus sunk into sleep and fell from a loft. Although those** *present considered Eutychus dead, Paul embraced him, discovering that Eutychus had survived (Acts 20:9-10 KJV).*

Q 21. (Acts 21) Who demanded to know Paul's identity during his arrest?

A 21. The chief captain made a command for Paul to be bound in chains and his identity revealed. He wanted to know what Paul had done. Before this, the Jews had removed Paul from the Temple and tried to kill him (Acts 21:30-33 KJV).

Q 22. (Acts 22) Who surrounded Paul (Saul) on his journey to Damascus?

A 22. A light in the presence of God surrounded Paul (Saul), who fell down. Paul (Saul) also heard Jesus' voice telling him to go to Damascus to learn God's plans for him (Acts 22:6-10 KJV).

Q 23. (Acts 23) Who many Jews made a conspiracy against Paul?

A 23. More than forty Jews conspired against Paul, saying they would not eat nor drink until they had killed him (Acts 23:12-13 KJV).

Q 24. (Acts 24) Who was Ananias, and who did he bring with him to accuse Paul?

A 24. Ananias was the high priest, and he brought elders and Tertullus, an orator, to inform the governor about Paul (Acts 24:1 KJV).

Q 25. (Acts 25) After the Jews made many accusations against Paul, Festus asked Paul if he would rather go to Jerusalem for his trial, and Paul requested to appeal to Caesar. Where did Festus send Paul?

A 25. Festus sent Paul to Caesar. In this way, Festus could please the Jews and avoid judging Paul himself (Acts 25:9, 12 KJV).

Q 26.   (Acts 26) At Paul's trial before King Agrippa, what did the king tell Paul he was permitted to do?

A 26.   *King Agrippa told Paul he could speak for himself, so Paul answered and told Agrippa he was happy to speak on his own behalf before the Jews made their accusations against him (Acts 26:1-2 KJV).*

Q 27.   (Acts 27) What was the name of the wind that struck the ship that could not withstand the storm?

A 27.   *The wind was called "Euroclydon" (Acts 27:14-15 KJV).*

Q 28.   (Acts 28) How long did Paul spend at the house he hired, and what did he do?

A 28.   *Paul spent two years at his hired house; confidently, Paul preached the kingdom of God and the Lord Jesus Christ to those who came; he did not receive any opposition (Acts 28:30-31 KJV).*

Score   /28 points

Questions and Answers - The Book of Romans

Q 1.   (Romans 1) Why is Paul eager to see the Romans?

A 1.   *Paul wants to give them a spiritual gift to establish them in Christ. Also, Paul and the Romans can comfort one another through their faith (Romans 1:11-12 KJV).*

Q 2.   (Romans 2) What happens to those who judge others?

A 2.   *Those who judge others condemn themselves because they do the same things. Paul reminds the Romans that God is the judge, and the basis of His judgment is truth (Romans 2:1-2 KJV).*

Q 3.   (Romans 3) How are sinners justified?

A 3.   *Because of His grace, God freely redeems those who have faith in Christ (Romans 3:24 KJV).*

Q 4.   (Romans 4) Which characters from the Scriptures does Paul refer to when speaking of righteousness?

A 4.   *Paul refers to Abraham and David, saying, "Abraham believed God, and it was counted unto him for righteousness." Then Paul added, "Even as David also describeth the blessedness of the man, unto whom God imputeth righteousness without works" (Romans 4:3, 6 KJV).*

Q 5.   (Romans 5) How do we obtain peace with God?

A 5.   *We obtain peace with God through faith in Christ. Having faith in Christ justifies sinners, leading to peace with God*

(Romans 5:1 KJV).

Q 6.   (Romans 6) Believers are dead to what?

A 6.   *Believers are dead to sin but alive in Christ; they identify with Christ's death and resurrection, becoming free from the power and control of sin to enjoy the newness of life (Romans 6:1-4 KJV).*

Q 7.   (Romans 7) According to the Law, what binds a woman to her husband?

A 7.   *The Law binds a woman to her husband as long as he is alive; if her husband dies, according to the Law, she is no longer bound (Romans 7:2 KJV).*

Q 8.   (Romans 8) According to Paul's teaching on life in the Spirit, who are the sons of God?

A 8.   *(Romans 8) Those led by God's Spirit are the sons of God. God's Spirit bears witness with their spirits; they become God's children (Romans 8:14-16 KJV).*

Q 9.   (Romans 9) Who said God would save a remnant of Israel?

A 9.   *Esaias (Isaiah) said God would save a remnant of Israel (Romans 9:27 KJV).*

Q 10.   (Romans 10) According to Paul, which righteousness did Moses describe?

A 10.   *Moses described the righteousness of the Law. However, to believers in Christ, the Law is not needed for righteousness (Romans 10:4-5 KJV).*

Q 11.   (Romans 11) How does Paul describe his heritage?

A 11.   *Paul says he is an Israelite from Abraham's seed and the tribe of Benjamin (Romans 11:1 KJV).*

Q 12.   (Romans 12) How does Paul tell the Romans to treat persecutors?

*A 12.   **Paul says to bless persecutors and not curse them (Romans 12:14 KJV).***

Q 13.   (Romans 13) What does Paul say about resisting the authority of higher powers?

*A 13.   **God ordains the rulers; those who resist God's ordinance and power will receive damnation (Romans 13:1-2 KJV).***

Q 14.   (Romans 14) Which things does Paul say we should seek?

*A 14.   **Paul says to seek things that bring peace and edify others (Romans 14:19 KJV).***

Q 15.   (Romans 15) What is Paul's reason for writing to the Romans?

*A 15.   **God gave Paul the grace to minister the Gospel of Christ to the Gentiles so that they could become an offering "sanctified by the Holy Ghost" (Romans 15:15-16 KJV).***

Q 16.   (Romans 16) Who does Paul commend unto the Romans, and what is his accolade for this person?

*A 16.   **Paul commends Phebe, who serves the church at Cenchrea; Paul asks the Romans to receive Phebe and help her in her church work as she has helped many beforehand (Romans 16:1-2 KJV).***

Score   /16 points

Questions and Answers - The Book of 1 Corinthians

Q 1.   (1 Corinthians 1) What caused Paul to implore those at Corinth to put aside contentions and join together?

A 1.   *Members of Chloe's household had informed Paul of divisions among the people. Paul's tone indicates an appeal for the Corinthians to join together in unity. Paul regards them as brothers in Christ, so he pleads with them to listen carefully and cease the divisions (1 Corinthians 1:10-11 KJV).*

Q 2.   (1 Corinthians 2) How does God reveal the deep things of God to those who love Him?

A 2.   *God reveals the wisdom of God through his Spirit. Believers know the things the Spirit reveals (1 Corinthians 2:10-12 KJV).*

Q 3.   (1 Corinthians 3) What example does Paul give of labouring together with God?

A 3.   *In Paul's example, he planted the seeds, Apollos watered them, but God caused them to grow. Without God causing the seeds to grow, planting and watering are fruitless acts (1 Corinthians 3:6-7 KJV).*

Q 4.   (1 Corinthians 4) How does Paul regard Timotheus (Timothy)?

A 4.   *Paul regards Timotheus (Timothy) as his "beloved son"; Paul knows Timotheus (Timothy) is a faithful follower of the Lord who shares in Christ's work (1 Corinthians 4:17 KJV).*

Q 5.   (1 Corinthians 5) Who does Paul identify as immoral?

A 5.   *Paul identifies fornicators, the covetous, idolaters, railers, drunkards, or extortioners; Paul's message is to avoid those who profess faith in Christ and still carry out these behaviors (1 Corinthians 5:11 KJV).*

_____

Q 6.   (1 Corinthians 6) What question does Paul raise regarding lawsuits among believers?

A 6.   *Paul asks the brethren if it would not be better to endure wrongdoing than enter into a lawsuit with another believer. He suggests it would be better to take the blame or suffer wrong (1 Corinthians 6:6-7 KJV).*

_____

Q 7.   (1 Corinthians 7) Should a woman or man leave an unbelieving spouse?

A 7.   *No. The believing spouse sanctifies the unbelieving spouse. Paul's teaching on marriage says the believing spouse has a godly impact on the unbeliever, making it possible for the unbeliever to convert; otherwise, their children would not become holy (1 Corinthians 7:14 KJV).*

_____

Q 8.   (1 Corinthians 8) What is Paul teaching about offering food to idols?

A 8.   *Idols have no value. Paul emphasizes that there is only one God and one Lord Jesus Christ. Offering food to idols is meaningless (1 Corinthians 8:4-6 KJV).*

_____

Q 9.   (1 Corinthians 9) What is the seal of Paul's apostleship?

A 9.   *Ministry with the people of Corinth in the Lord is Paul's seal. Others may doubt that Paul is an apostle, but there is evidence at Corinth of Paul's apostleship (1 Corinthians 9:2 KJV).*

_____

Q 10.   (1 Corinthians 10) What does Paul teach about temptation?

A 10.   *Temptation comes to all. However, God will not allow temptation beyond that which we can bear, and He will provide a
means of escape, making it possible to endure the temptation
(1 Corinthians 10:13 KJV).*

Q 11.   (1 Corinthians 11) According to Paul, how should a woman pray and
prophesize?

A 11.   *A woman's head should be covered when she prays or proph-
esizes; otherwise, she humiliates herself as though she had
shaved her head (1 Corinthians 11:5-6 KJV).*

Q 12.   (1 Corinthians 12) What does Paul say about spiritual gifts?

A 12.   *Believers receive diverse gifts that perform different func-
tions, but one Spirit and one God works in all of these gifts (1
Corinthians 12:4-6 KJV).*

Q 13.   (1 Corinthians 13) What will never fail?

A 13.   *Charity will never fail; it is kind and not envious or boastful
(1 Corinthians 13:4, 8 KJV).*

Q 14.   (1 Corinthians 14) What does Paul say about "speaking in tongues"
and prophesying?

A 14.   *"Speaking in tongues" edifies the one who speaks, but prophesying edifies the church. Paul adds that prophecy is greater
than speaking in tongues, but if an interpretation of "speaking in tongues" takes place, it edifies the church (1 Corinthians 14:4-5 KJV).*

Q 15.   (1 Corinthians 15) Who first saw Jesus after the resurrection?

A 15.   *Cephas first saw Jesus, and the disciples saw Him next (1
Corinthians 15:5 KJV).*

Q 16.   (1 Corinthians 16) What instructions does Paul give the church of
Galatia and Corinth at the end of the epistle?

*A 16.   At the end of the epistle, Paul tells the Corinthians to set
aside a collection for the poor; Paul tells them to set apart
this amount on the first day of the week (1Corinthians 16:1-2
KJV).*

_____

Score   /16 points

Questions and Answers - The Book of 2 Corinthians

Q 1.   (2 Corinthians 1) How does Paul explain God's comfort?

A 1.   *God comforts us in our tribulations so that we can comfort others; Paul describes God as "the God of all comfort" (2 Corinthians 1:3-4 KJV).*

Q 2.   (2 Corinthians 2) How should the church respond to those who have caused grief or offense?

A 2.   *Paul teaches believers to forgive, comfort, and demonstrate love toward those who have caused grief or offense. He points out that they have received enough punishment and appeals to the church to love them (2 Corinthians 2:5-8 KJV).*

Q 3.   (2 Corinthians 3) What does Paul say about God's sufficiency?

A 3.   *Paul says we should not think too highly of ourselves as God is our sufficiency; without God, we can accomplish nothing (2 Corinthians 3:5 KJV).*

Q 4.   (2 Corinthians 4) What happens to the minds of those who do not believe in Christ?

A 4.   *Satan keeps the minds of unbelievers from accepting the truth of Christ; their minds cannot see the truth (2 Corinthians 4:4 KJV).*

Q 5.   (2 Corinthians 5) Paul discusses the concept of judgment. What will happen to every believer at the judgment seat of Christ?

A 5. **All believers in Christ will account for things they have done, good and bad (2 Corinthians 5:10 KJV).**

Q 6.   (2 Corinthians 6) How does Paul describe believers in verse 16?

A 6. **Paul says, "for ye are the temple of the living God" (2 Corinthians 6:16 KJV).**

Q 7.   (2 Corinthians 7) How did Paul receive good news in Macedonia?

A 7. **God comforted Paul through the arrival of Titus, who brought good news, causing Paul to rejoice. Paul arrived in Macedonia amid troubles, fighting, and fears. However, God provided comfort through the arrival of Titus and the consolation of the people of Corinth (2 Corinthians 7:5-7 KJV).**

Q 8.   (2 Corinthians 8) How does Paul describe Titus' ministry?

A 8. **Paul describes Titus as his "partner and fellowhelper" to emphasize their joint ministry; Paul will not be at Corinth, but Titus will diligently carry out the work of the Lord (2 Corinthians 8:22-23 KJV).**

Q 9.   (2 Corinthians 9) What kind of giver does God love?

A 9. **God loves a cheerful giver who gives freely from the heart (2 Corinthians 9:7 KJV).**

Q 10.   (2 Corinthians 10) What does Paul say about our weapons?

A 10. **Paul says they are not carnal because they contain the power of God that can demolish strongholds (2 Corinthians 10:4 KJV).**

Q 11.   (2 Corinthians 11) How many shipwrecks did Paul survive?

A 11. **Paul suffered three shipwrecks in which he spent a day and night upon deep waters (2 Corinthians 11:25 KJV).**

Q 12.   (2 Corinthians 12) What is Paul's appeal to the Corinthians?

A 12. *Paul urges those who have committed sexual sin to repent (2 Corinthians 12:21).*

_____

Q 13.   (2 Corinthians 13) What command does Paul make to the Corinthians when ending the epistle?

A 13. *Paul commands them to examine and prove themselves to know they have Christ's presence. An obedient Christian can feel Christ's presence (2 Corinthians 13:5 KJV).*

_____

Score   /13 points

Questions and Answers - The Book of Galatians

Q 1.   (Galatians 1) Paul certifies that he did not receive the Gospel he preached from man or through man's teaching. How did Paul receive the Gospel?

A 1.   *Jesus Christ revealed the Gospel to Paul so he could convert the Gentiles. Paul's authority came from God, and he did not confer with man about it (Galatians 1:11-12, 16 KJV).*

Q 2.   (Galatians 2) What evidence does Paul give that the church accepted him?

A 2.   *Church leaders James, Cephas, and John gave Paul and Barnabas "the right hands of fellowship"; they recognized Paul's calling and confirmed their ministry to the Jews and Paul's ministry to the Gentiles (Galatians 2:9 KJV).*

Q 3.   (Galatians 3) Who does Paul say could also receive the blessing Abraham received from God?

A 3.   *Through faith in Christ, the Gentiles could also receive the blessing Abraham received and the promise of the Spirit; Christ's grace makes it possible for all who place their faith in Him to receive the promise of the Spirit (Galatians 3:14 KJV).*

Q 4.   (Galatians 4) What did Paul tell the Galatians about freedom from bondage?

A 4.   *Paul told them that at one time, they were in bondage under the Law. However, when the time came, God sent Christ to*

*redeem them from the Law, allowing them to become sons
and heirs of God. God sent "the Spirit of his Son into their
hearts, crying Abba, Father" (Galatians 4:3-7 KJV).*

Q 5.   (Galatians 5) Which warning does Paul give the Galatians?

A 5.   *Paul's warning is to avoid entanglement with the yoke of
bondage. Christ set them free of the Law, so Paul tells them
not to return to it as it will keep them in bondage (Galatians
5:1 KJV).*

Q 6.   (Galatians 6) Where was Paul when he wrote to the Galatians?

A 6.   *Paul was in Rome (Galatians 6:18 KJV).*

Score   /6 points

Questions and Answers - The Book of Ephesians

Q 1.   (Ephesians 1) What had Paul heard about the Ephesians?

A 1.   *Paul heard about the Ephesians' faith in Jesus and love for the saints; he gives thanks for the Ephesians and prays that God would give them wisdom and the knowledge of God (Ephesians 1:15-17 KJV).*

Q 2.   (Ephesians 2) How does God quicken us?

A 2.   *God quickens us together with Christ when we put our faith in Him, and He saves us by His grace. When sinners put their faith in Christ, God saves them through Christ and raises them to new life (Ephesians 2:4-6 KJV).*

Q 3.   (Ephesians 3) How does Paul describe the gift of God's grace he received?

A 3.   *Paul received God's grace to preach to the Gentiles "the un-searchable riches of Christ" (Ephesians 3:8 KJV).*

Q 4.   (Ephesians 4) According to Paul, who walks in vanity?

A 4.   *Paul tells the Ephesians that the Gentiles walk in the vanity of their minds with blinded hearts by living apart from God (Ephesians 4:17-18 KJV).*

Q 5.   (Ephesians 5) How does Paul say men should love their wives?

A 5.   *Paul tells them to love their wives the way they love their own bodies; he adds that by loving their wives, they also love themselves (Ephesians 5:28 KJV).*

Q 6.   (Ephesians 6) What command does Paul give children, and what
        does he say will be the result of following this command?

A 6.   *Children should honour and obey their parents. As a result,
        they will live long lives (Ephesians 6:1-3 KJV).*

Score   /6 points

Questions and Answers - The Book of Philippians

Q 1.   (Philippians 1) With Timotheus (Timothy), who does Paul address at Philippi, and what does he desire?

A 1.   *Paul addresses the saints, bishops, and deacons at Philippi, desiring that they will have grace and peace from God and our Lord Jesus Christ (Philippians 1:1-2 KJV).*

Q 2.   (Philippians 2) How does Paul tell the Philippians to live in a corrupt society?

A 2.   *Paul tells the Philippians they live amid crookedness and perversity, reminding them of the surrounding wickedness. He says they must live up to their duty, shine their lights for Christ, and live as sons of God without blame or harm (Philippians 2:15 KJV).*

Q 3.   (Philippians 3) Finish this verse: "I press toward the mark _____" (Philippians 3:14 KJV).

A 3.   *"I press toward the mark for the prize of the high calling of God in Christ Jesus" (Philippians 3:14 KJV).*

Q 4.   (Philippians 4) What does Paul communicate to the Philippians
         about their gift-giving toward his ministry?

A 4.   *Paul reminds the Philippians that they gave him gifts to help*
           with his needs when he left Macedonia and Thessalonica. He
           adds that it is not the gifts he values but wants them to receive
           the fruits of their gifts and sacrifices. Paul ends by stating
           his confidence that God will provide them with all they need
           through Christ (Philippians 4:15-19 KJV).

_____

Score   /4 points

Questions and Answers - The Book of Colossians

Q 1.   (Colossians 1) How does Paul's prayer for the Colossians begin and
        end?

A 1.   ***Initially, Paul prays for the Colossians to obtain knowledge
        of Gods' wisdom. His prayer ends with a reminder that God
        took them out of darkness into Christ's kingdom, providing
        redemption and forgiveness of sin through Christ's blood
        (Colossians 1:9, 13-14 KJV).***

Q 2.   (Colossians 2) How does Paul describe the sufficiency of Christ?

A 2.   ***Christ is truly God, so He is all we need. Christ is sufficient
        for us, making us complete in Him (Colossians 2:9-10 KJV).***

Q 3.   (Colossians 3) What does Paul tell the Colossians to avoid?

A 3.   ***Paul tells the Colossians not to focus on earthly things but
        to keep their hearts on things above; Christ is in Heaven, so
        that is where they should set their affections (Colossians 3:1-
        2 KJV).***

Q 4.   (Colossians 4) In Paul's final words to the Colossians, what request
        does he make regarding the epistles?

A 4.   *Paul would like the epistle read at the church of the La-*
        odiceans; also, he would like the Colossians to read the
        epistle from the Laodiceans. He ends the epistle asking the
        Colossians to remind Archippus to fulfil his call to ministry
        (Colossians 4:16-17 KJV).

_____

Score   /4 points

Questions and Answers - The Book of 1 Thessalonians

Q 1.   (1 Thessalonians 1) Where did the Thessalonians spread the Lord's Word?

A 1.   ***The Thessalonians spread the Lord's Word in Macedonia, Achaia, and abroad. They responded to the Gospel and vigorously spread the message (1 Thessalonians 1:7- 8 KJV).***

Q 2.   (1 Thessalonians 2) Which words did Paul not use while carrying out God's work in Thessalonica?

A 2.   ***Paul presented the truth without using flattering words because God trusted him with the Gospel, so he wanted his message to please God, not men (1 Thessalonians 2:4-5 KJV).***

Q 3.   (1 Thessalonians 3) Why did Paul send Timotheus (Timothy) to Thessalonica?

A 3.   ***Paul sent him to Thessalonica to establish and comfort the Thessalonians in their afflictions. Paul felt the need to stay in Athens, so he sent Timotheus (Timothy), his brother in Christ (1 Thessalonians 3:1-3 KJV).***

Q 4.   (1 Thessalonians 4) When the Lord descends, what will happen to the dead who are in Christ, and what will happen afterward?

A 4.   ***The dead who are in Christ will rise first. Then, those alive will meet them to spend eternity with God (1 Thessalonians 4:16-17 KJV).***

Q 5.   (1 Thessalonians 5) Where was Paul when he wrote 1
        Thessalonians?

A 5.   Paul was in Athens (1 Thessalonians 5:28 KJV).

Score   /5 points

Questions and Answers - The Book of 2 Thessalonians

Q 1.   (2 Thessalonians 1) What does Paul say will happen to those who do not know God or obey Christ's Gospel?

A 1.   *"In flaming fire," God will punish them with eternal destruction from God's presence and glorious power (2 Thessalonians 1:8-9 KJV).*

Q 2.   (2 Thessalonians 2) How does Paul feel toward the Thessalonians?

A 2.   *Paul is thankful for the Thessalonians; God chose and sanctified them through the Holy Spirit and their faith (2 Thessalonians 2:13 KJV).*

Q 3.   (2 Thessalonians 3) What command does Paul make about associating with the disorderly?

A 3.   *Paul commands the Thessalonians to withdraw from brothers who walk in a disorderly way (2 Thessalonians 3:6 KJV).*

Score   /3 points

Questions and Answers - The Book of 1 Timothy

Questions and Answers

Q 1.　(1 Timothy 1) When Paul went to Macedonia, why did he tell Timothy to stay at Ephesus?

A 1.　*Paul wanted Timothy to remain at Ephesus to end the teaching of false doctrines that was taking place there, causing disagreements that did not edify God (1 Timothy 1:3-4 KJV).*

Q 2.　(1 Timothy 2) What does Paul exhort as a pattern for prayer?

A 2.　*Paul encourages "supplications, prayers, intercessions, and giving of thanks" for everyone and those in authority so peace and honesty can exist among the people (1 Timothy 2:1-2 KJV).*

Q 3.　(1 Timothy 3) How should a bishop rule his home?

A 3.　*A bishop should rule his household diligently and raise obedient, respectful children (1 Timothy 3:4 KJV).*

Q 4.　(1 Timothy 4) What does Paul tell Timothy to do as a leader until he visits?

A 4.　*Paul tells Timothy to pay attention to reading, exhortation, and doctrine and use the spiritual gifts already confirmed through prophecy and "the laying on of hands" by other leaders (1 Timothy 4:13-14 KJV).*

Q 5.　(1 Timothy 5) What does Paul say about the care of widows?

A 5.   ***Paul recognizes that widows may need care and emphasizes that their families should take responsibility toward caring for them as this is favorable to God (1 Timothy 5:3-4 KJV).***

Q 6.   (1 Timothy 6) What was the chief city of Phrygia?

A 6.   ***The chief city of Phrygia Pacatiana was Laodicea (1 Timothy 6:21 KJV).***

Score   /6 points

Questions and Answers - The Book of 2 Timothy

Q 1.   (2 Timothy 1) When Paul encourages Timothy to remain faithful, whose faith does he recall?

A 1.   Paul acknowledges Timothy's grandmother Lois and his mother Eunice; Paul is confident that Timothy possesses true faith. Paul uses this opportunity to remind Timothy to grow and develop his spiritual gift (2 Timothy 1:5-6 KJV).

Q 2.   (2 Timothy 2) What does Paul tell Timothy about being a workman?

A 2.   Paul says, "Study to shew thyself approved unto God, a workman that needeth not to be ashamed, rightly dividing the word of truth" (2 Timothy 2:15 KJV).

Q 3.   (2 Timothy 3) What does Paul tell Timothy about the godliness that will exist during the last days?

A 3.   The last days will be perilous, according to Paul; there will be an appearance of godliness but denial and avoidance of the power of God. Paul describes a time to come when some will cease to follow God and live corrupt lives (2 Timothy 3:1-9 KJV).

Q 4.   (2 Timothy 4) Where did Paul send Tychicus?

A 4.   ***Paul sent Tychicus to Ephesus (2 Timothy 4:12 KJV).***

Score   **/4 points**

Questions and Answers - The Book of Titus

Q 1.   (Titus 1) What was Titus' task in Crete?

A 1.   Paul left Titus at Crete to rectify problems and ordain elders in the cities. He also states that the elders should have good character, one wife, and well-behaved children of faith (Titus 1:5-6 KJV).

Q 2.   (Titus 2) Who does Paul say should be sober-minded?

A 2.   Young men should be sober-minded, according to Paul's teaching (Titus 2:6 KJV).

Q 3.   (Titus 3) What should be the attitude toward heretics, according to Paul?

A 3.   Paul says to admonish heretics twice then reject them; they are corrupt sinners who condemn themselves. (Titus 3:10-11 KJV).

Score   /3 points

Questions and Answers - The Book of Philemon

Question and Answer

Q 1.   (Philemon) What is Paul's appeal to Philemon about his former servant, Onesimus, who wronged him?

A 1.   Paul appeals to Philemon to accept Onesimus in the same way he would accept Paul himself. Paul's bond to Onesimus is so strong that he is willing to pay Onesimus' past debts. To Paul, Onesimus is a beloved Christian brother, and he would like Philemon to forget Onesimus' mistake and move onward with his brother in Christ (Philemon 8-21 KJV).

Score   /1 point

Questions and Answers - The Book of Hebrews

Q 1.   (Hebrews 1) How did God speak in times past, and how did He
        speak in later times?

A 1.   *God previously spoke through the prophets, but later He
        spoke through His son, Jesus, "heir of all things" (Hebrews
        1:1-2 KJV).*

Q 2.   (Hebrews 2) According to Hebrews 2:18, what is one reason Jesus
        suffered temptation?

A 2.   *Christ suffered temptation to show us how to deal with temp-
        tation in our lives (Hebrews 2:18 KJV).*

Q 3.   (Hebrews 3) According to the author of Hebrews, what kept some
        from entering into Christ's rest?

A 3.   *Those who could not enter Christ's rest did not believe in
        Christ. When those with hardened hearts grieved the Lord
        because of unbelief, the Lord said they would not enter His
        rest (Hebrews 3:17-19 KJV).*

Q 4.   (Hebrews 4) How does Christ provide a way to God?

A 4.   *Through Christ, we can go boldly to God's Throne to find
        mercy and grace. Christ is the way to God (Hebrews 4:16
        KJV).*

Q 5.   (Hebrews 5) Who was Melchisedek (Melchizedek)?

A 5.   *Melchisedek (Melchizedek) was a high priest and King of*

Salem. As a high priest, Melchisedek (Melchizedek) blessed Abraham (Hebrews 5:10 KJV; Genesis 14:18-20 KJV).

Q 6.   (Hebrews 6) According to the author of Hebrews, who received the promise of God?

A 6.   *God promised to bless and multiply Abraham, which he did. Abraham waited patiently and received God's promise (Hebrews 6:13-15 KJV).*

Q 7.   (Hebrews 7) What did Abraham give Melchisedek (Melchizedek)?

A 7.   *Abraham gave Melchisedek (Melchizedek) one-tenth of his spoils; Melchisedek (Melchizedek) blessed Abraham when he met him coming from the slaughter of the kings (Hebrews 7:1-4 KJV).*

Q 8.   (Hebrews 8) Where is our high priest?

A 8.   *Our high priest sits at the right hand of God in Heaven (Hebrews 8:1 KJV).*

Q 9.   (Hebrews 9) How does the author describe Christ's sacrifice?

A 9.   *The author says that Christ sacrificed His life to cover sin for many, and He will appear again to those who trust in Him (Hebrews 9:28 KJV).*

Q 10.   (Hebrews 10) What does the author say about the daily sacrifices the priests offer?

A 10.   *The author says that although the priests offer daily sacrifices, they cannot take away sins. Christ's sacrifice, made once, covered sin forever (Hebrews 10:11-12 KJV).*

Q 11.   (Hebrews 11) Who are the first three examples of faith discussed in Hebrews 11?

A 11.   *Abel, Enoch, and Noah are the first three examples of faith in this passage. Abel obtained righteousness for offering a better sacrifice than Cain, Enoch did not die but went to Heaven because he pleased God, and when Noah built the ark, he became righteous due to his faith (Hebrews 11:4-7 KJV).*

Q 12.   (Hebrews 12) Where is Mount Sion (Zion)?

A 12.   *It is in Jerusalem (Hebrews 12:22 KJV).*

Q 13.   (Hebrews 13) Why is it essential to entertain strangers?

A 13.   *It is important to entertain strangers because they might be angels. The author reminds the Hebrews that some have experienced angels without knowing who they were (Hebrews 13:2 KJV).*

Score   /13 points

Questions and Answers - The Book of James

Q 1.   (James 1) Who deceives themselves, according to James?

A 1.   *James says those who hear the Word but do nothing deceive themselves; they are like a man who sees his face in a glass, goes away, and forgets how he looked (James 1:22-24 KJV).*

Q 2.   (James 2) Who does James point to as examples of those justified by faith?

A 2.   *To emphasize the faith of Abraham and Rahab, James asks if Abraham were not justified when he offered Isaac, his son, on an altar, and if Rahab's works did not prove her faith when she received the spies and helped them escape (James 2:21, 25 KJV).*

Q 3.   (James 3) The tongue is full of what, according to James?

A 3.   *It contains "deadly poison" (James 3:8 KJV).*

Q 4.   (James 4) What does James say happens when we draw close to God?

A 4.   *When we walk closely with God, He draws close to us (James 4:8 KJV).*

Q 5.   (James 5) What happened when Elias (Elijah) prayed that it would not rain, and what happened when he prayed again? Who does Elias (Elijah) represent to James?

A 5.   *First, Elias (Elijah) prayed it would not rain, and it did not*

*rain for many years. However, when Elias (Elijah) prayed
again, it rained. To James, Elias (Elijah) represents one who
prayed earnestly and received results (James 5:16-18 KJV).*

Score   /5 points

Questions and Answers - The Book of 1 Peter

Q 1.   (1 Peter 1) Which similes does Peter use to describe flesh?

A 1.   *Using similes, Peter says, "For all flesh is as grass, and all the glory of man as the flower of grass. The grass withereth, and the flower thereof falleth away: /But the word of the Lord endureth for ever. And this is the word which by the gospel is preached unto you" (1 Peter 1:24-25 KJV).*

Q 2.   (1 Peter 2) How does Peter describe Christ?

A 2.   *Peter refers to Scripture that describes Christ as our rock or solid foundation on whom we can depend: "Behold, I lay in Sion a chief corner stone, elect, precious: and he that believeth on him shall not be confounded" (1 Peter 2:6 KJV).*

Q 3.   (1 Peter 3) According to 1 Peter 3:8, what traits should Christians display?

A 3.   *Christians should show compassion, love, pity, and courtesy (1 Peter 3:8 KJV).*

Q 4.   (1 Peter 4) What does Peter say about showing hospitality?

A 4.   *Peter says to show hospitality as good stewards and pass along the gifts we receive from God to others without grudging (1 Peter 4:9-10 KJV).*

Q 5.   (1 Peter 5) What does Peter say we should do with our cares?

A 5.   **Peter says we should cast our cares upon God who cares for us (1 Peter 5:7 KJV).**

_____

Score   /5 points

Questions and Answers - The Book of 2 Peter

Q 1.   (2 Peter 1) How did prophecy arise, according to Peter?

A 1.   *Peter makes it clear that the prophets received their words from God. Holy men spoke as the Holy Spirit moved them to speak (2 Peter 1:20-21 KJV).*

Q 2.   (2 Peter 2) Whose ass (donkey) spoke?

A 2.   *Balaam's ass (donkey) spoke (2 Peter 2:16 KJV).*

Q 3.   (2 Peter 3) How does Peter describe Christ's return?

A 3.   *"But the day of the Lord will come as a thief in the night; in the which the heavens shall pass away with a great noise, and the elements shall melt with fervent heat, the earth also and the works that are therein shall be burned up" (2 Peter 3:10).*

Score   /3 points

Questions and Answers - The Book of 1 John

Q 1.   (1 John 1) According to John, what happens when we say we do not sin?

A 1.   *We deceive ourselves, and we do not tell the truth (1 John 1:8-9 KJV).*

Q 2.   (1 John 2) Who abides in the light, according to John?

A 2.   *Those who love their brothers live in the light, but those who hate their brothers live in darkness. The darkness blinds their eyes, so they do not know the right way to go (1 John 2:10-11 KJV).*

Q 3.   (1 John 3) Which commandments of Christ does John speak about at the end of this chapter?

A 3.   *John says that by keeping Christ's commandments and pleasing Him, we receive what we ask. Christ commanded us to believe in Jesus Christ and love each other (1 John 3:22-23 KJV).*

Q 4.   (1 John 4) What is a man who says he loves God but hates his brother?

A 4.   *God commands His followers to love their brothers. The man who says he loves God but hates his brother is a "liar" (1 John 4:20-21 KJV).*

Q 5.   (1 John 5) At the end of the epistle, what warning does John give his audience?

A 5.   John tells his audience to avoid idols (1 John 5:21 KJV).

Score   /5 points

Questions and Answers - The Book of 2 John

Q 1.   (2 John) In this chapter, what is the meaning of love?

A 1.   **Love means walking after the commandments of Christ. John repeats the commandment given from the beginning to love one another (2 John 5-6 KJV).**

Score   /1 point

Questions and Answers - The Book of 3 John

Q 1.   (3 John) Who does John address?

A 1.   *The author addresses Gaius (3 John 1 KJV).*

_____

Score   /1 point

Questions and Answers - The Book of Jude

Q 1.   (Jude) What appeal does Jude make in verse 3?

A 1.   *Jude makes an appeal to contend diligently for the faith that*
        the saints received. He says to do the utmost to keep the faith
        in the Lord Jesus Christ (Jude 3 KJV).

        _____

        Score   /1 point

Questions and Answers - The Book of Revelation

Q 1.   (Revelation 1) Jesus is the source of the revelation John received for the seven churches. How did the revelation come to John?

A 1.   *John heard a voice that told him to record his vision and send it to the seven churches in Asia: Ephesus, Smyrna, Pergamos, Thyatira, Sardis, Philadelphia, and Laodicea. John saw the Son of Man amid seven candlesticks (Revelation 1:10-13 KJV).*

Q 2.   (Revelation 2) Why did John's message tell the church at Ephesus to repent?

A 2.   *Despite the works, labour, and patience of those at the church of Ephesus, they were in danger of losing their position as they no longer shone their lights for Christ. The church at Ephesus had left its "first love" (Revelation 2:3-5 KJV).*

Q 3.   (Revelation 3) What was the problem with the church at Laodicea?

A 3.   *The church at Laodicea was in danger of abandonment by God as they did not see the need for Christ because of their riches and material goods. The church at Laodicea was "lukewarm" (Revelation 3:16-17 KJV).*

Q 4.   (Revelation 4) What did John see surrounding the Throne in Heaven?

A 4.   *A rainbow that looked like an emerald surrounded the Throne (Revelation 4:3 KJV).*

Q 5.   (Revelation 5) John saw the Son of Man sitting on a Throne holding a book. An angel asked who was worthy to open the book. Which men could open the book?

A 5.   *Not one man in Heaven, on earth, or under the earth could open the book as they were not worthy to even look into the book (Revelation 5:3-4 KJV).*

Q 6.   (Revelation 6) When John saw the Lamb opening the sixth seal, an earthquake took place, the sun turned black, and the moon looked like blood. What happened to the stars?

A 6.   *The stars fell to the earth (Revelation 6:13 KJV).*

Q 7.   (Revelation 7) How many of God's servants did the angels seal?

A 7.   *The servants sealed one hundred forty-four thousand of God's servants in their foreheads (Revelation 7:3-4 KJV).*

Q 8.   (Revelation 8) What happened when John saw the Lamb opening the seventh seal?

A 8.   *Heaven was silent for half an hour. John saw seven angels standing in front of God; the angels had seven trumpets (Revelation 8:1-2 KJV).*

Q 9.   (Revelation 9) Who received the key of "the bottomless pit"?

A 9.   *The star received the key and opened the bottomless pit that emitted smoke. Locusts arose in the smoke, but they could only harm those who did not have God's seal (Revelation 9:1-4 KJV).*

Q 10.   (Revelation 10) What happened when John asked the angel for the little book?

A 10.   *The angel told John to "eat the book." It was sweet in his mouth and bitter in his belly (Revelation 10:9-10 KJV).*

Q 11.   (Revelation 11) How did John describe the reed?

A 11.   John said the reed was "like unto a rod," and he received a command from the angel to measure the temple, the altar, and the worshippers (Revelation 11:1 KJV).

Q 12.   (Revelation 12) Who fought the dragon during the war in Heaven?

A 12.   Michael and his angels did, casting the dragon and his angels out of Heaven (Revelation 12:7-9 KJV).

Q 13.   (Revelation 13) What restrictions did the beast place on those who did not receive the mark?

A 13.   Those who did not have the mark, name of the beast, or its number could not buy and sell (Revelation 13:17 KJV).

Q 14.   (Revelation 14) Who did John see standing on Mount Sion (Zion), and who was with Him? What appeared on their foreheads?

A 14.   A Lamb stood there, and there were a hundred forty-four thousand with Him. On their foreheads was His Father's name (Revelation 14:1 KJV).

Q 15.   (Revelation 15) What did one of the beasts give the seven angels?

A 15.   The beast gave the angels seven vials filled with God's wrath (Revelation 15:7 KJV).

Q 16.   (Revelation 16) What happened to the islands and mountains in Revelation 16:20?

A 16.   The islands "fled away," and the mountains disappeared (Revelation 16:20 KJV).

Q 17.   (Revelation 17) When the Spirit took John to the wilderness, what did John see?

A 17.   John saw a woman sitting on a red-colored beast with blas-

phemous names and seven heads; it also had ten horns (Revelation 17:3 KJV).

Q 18. (Revelation 18) John saw an angel who told him that the city of Babylon had fallen. How long did it take for the city to fall?

A 18. It took one hour, and the shipmasters and sailors cried out at the desolation (Revelation 18:17-19 KJV).

Q 19. (Revelation 19) What happened to the beast in Revelation 19:20?

A 19. God cast the beast "into a lake of fire" that burned with brimstone (Revelation 19:20 KJV).

Q 20. (Revelation 20) What did the angel coming from Heaven have in his hand?

A 20. Carrying the key to the bottomless pit and a chain, the angel bound the dragon, cast him into the bottomless pit, and sealed him for a thousand years (Revelation 20:1-3 KJV).

Q 21. (Revelation 21) To whom does John compare Jerusalem?

A 21. John compares Jerusalem to a bride prepared for her husband (Revelation 21:2 KJV).

Q 22. (Revelation 22) What does John say will happen to those who add to his prophecy?

A 22. God will send the plagues described in the book to those who add to the prophecy (Revelation 22:18 KJV).

Score /22 points   Total: /260 points